Principles of Likability:
Skills for a Memorable First Impression, Captivating Presence, and Instant Friendships

By Patrick King
Social Interaction Specialist and
Conversation Coach
www.PatrickKingConsulting.com

Table of Contents

Principles of Likability: Skills for a Memorable First Impression, Captivating Presence, and Instant Friendships.................. 3

Table of Contents 5

Introduction 7

Chapter 1: The Principle of Deciding to Be Friends.. 13

Chapter 2: The Principle of Self-Disclosure 37

Chapter 3: The Principle of Safety and Comfort... 67

Chapter 4: The Principle of Listening 85

Chapter 5: The Principle of Being Valuable 111

Chapter 6: The Principle of Shallowness 125

Chapter 7: The Principle of Empathy 139

Chapter 8: The Principle of Abrasiveness 153

Chapter 9: The Principle of Worthiness.. 177

Cheat Sheet.. 195

Introduction

One of my friends Yuval came to me with a curious complaint a couple of years ago. He had recently moved to a new city and was having trouble making friends. I told him to give it some time, but he reminded me that it had been over a year and he still had made no progress, so I started to suspect he was doing something wrong.

I had known him since we were toddlers, so it was hard for me to say what it could be. After all, when you're a toddler, you don't necessarily stroll to the sandbox with the intention of making lifelong friends. More likely, we met in the sandbox and fought for the same toy truck, then ended up spending time together because of our constant clashes. The point is, I had no context for how Yuval was making friends or making himself likable to others.

Naturally, I asked him what steps he was taking to create a new social circle. He told me he was meeting people all the time, but no one ever seemed to invite him out. His coworkers did only seldomly, and people he met at hobby groups, group events, or from his Frisbee golf team didn't seem to either. From this one answer, I knew what his problem was; he was putting the burden of taking initiative on everyone else but him. He made the mistake of assuming that, since no one was actively making an effort to include him, he wasn't welcome. He was disempowering himself by thinking that he needed to wait for others to make the first step and that he didn't have the power to initiate himself.

He didn't understand that to make new friends, and especially to break into existing social circles, *he* was the one that needed to make the effort to reach out, follow up, invite, and plan. He needed to be the one showing up and making things happen because, frankly, most people are either too lazy or too passive to make new friends as often as they can. People fall into routines and find their small enclaves and don't often explore outside of them, so Yuval needed to generate enough momentum to either find people who were more open or break into those enclaves.

Expecting anything else is like sitting at home in the dark and being surprised when you discover that you don't have a nice tan. Yuval adjusted his behavior—all it really required was initiating three more text conversations a week—and was able to find his own enclave in his new city soon enough.

I didn't realize it at the time, but Yuval was the victim of the thought process that keeps many of us from new friends and easy likability. He decided to treat people like they weren't friends yet, which means he treated them like strangers. This meant some version of formality between a job interview and a professional networking event. Not very conducive to the impression most of us want to present to new friends.

It turns out, making the small decision to be friends and skip the unnecessary progression of slowly warming up to people is a major key in how likable you are. Likability is not rocket science, but there are specific principles I've found through my own experience, my years coaching, and my hawk-like observation of people that tip the scales. Thankfully, the principles I've described in this book aren't things you need to be born with; they are behaviors you can cultivate and grow.

When people like you, they are happy to do favors for you and provide you with whatever you might need. They show you brand new opportunities and open doors for your success. As social animals, humans crave companionship and friendship, and you'll never be lacking in that. The world is not a meritocracy, unfortunately, and likability is an everyday superpower that can grant you the keys to any situation.

Chapter 1: The Principle of Deciding to Be Friends

Charlie is a standoffish guy. He doesn't like to talk to people he doesn't know. When he is introduced to Michael, he keeps his usual cold distance. This makes Michael think that Charlie doesn't like him. Michael doesn't count Charlie as a friend and avoids him since being around Charlie makes him feel disliked and uncomfortable. Meanwhile, Charlie actually desperately wants to become friends with Michael and wonders why Michael doesn't see his continued interaction as a sign of interest.

Let's imagine if Charlie took a different approach to strangers and even acquaintances.

What if when he met Michael, he decided to be warm and make the conscious decision to become friends with Michael? Off the bat, he considers Michael a close friend. He would be beyond shallow small talk and genuinely care about what is going on in his life. His efforts would pay off because they make Michael open up and feel engaged. Michael starts to talk to Charlie and they find things in common that help them establish a good friendship.

Initially, Charlie didn't think of Michael as a friend and it became a reality. Charlie's mindset made him treat Michael as a stranger, and Michael reciprocated within the tone that was set. But thinking of Michael as a friend made Charlie treat him as such. This seems like such an easy choice to make, but this isn't how we are conditioned to think about people.

Make the Conscious Decision

We're conditioned to think about people from a linear perspective. Introduce self, sniff them out, determine their worth, and then slowly invest in building a relationship. But that's wrong for so many reasons. This creates the very mindset that keeps you from being likable and making friends—it creates a path for hoops for people to jump through. What happens when we follow the linear path and treat people like a stranger?

People erect walls around strangers. They have been taught to do this to protect themselves, since you can never know what another person's intentions are if you are too blindly trusting. The coldness and distance you put out will drive the other person away, preventing friendship from budding. Simply realizing that you are acting in two completely different ways should allow you to see the better decision to make—the decision to treat people as friends instantly. Someone has to make the first step, and it might as well be you.

It's a matter of small shifts in thought—for instance, the difference between saying "We're friends" or "We're not friends yet." Your behavior toward someone adjusts as you adopt one of those attitudes. If you say "We're friends," warmth is immediately established and you let your guard down and don't converse as if you are in a job interview.

When you say "We're not friends yet," you keep people at an arm's length. This distance is chilly and can be off-putting to the other person. You feel like something needs to happen, a sign of some sort, for you to relax and be yourself. You are reserved and bite your tongue and generally don't reveal your real personality.

For example, when you meet a new neighbor, you can go one of two ways. You can treat him as a stranger and get to know him gradually through a series of boring conversations over weeks. Your neighbor sees no reason to like you or engage with you, so he doesn't. Or you could go the other way and make the decision to act like old friends, ignore conventional barriers, and invite him into your life. Now you two are buddies and he is more than willing to watch your house when you are gone and feed your elderly cats. How you choose to regard this neighbor dictates your behavior and hence dictates your future relationship and interactions.

Think about the way you physically regard friends. Friends are not distant in any way, shape, or form. They will touch each other and hug goodbye. They will violate the strict physical and mental distance boundaries that people naturally erect in the face of something unfamiliar.

Again, consider the body language and background tension that will linger over a job interview, or simply even two strangers having lunch. But if you observe a meal between two friends, you'll see people with their guards down, touching, violating space, and probably violating each other's privacy repeatedly. They joke around and bring up personal details that they know about each other. Their body language is more relaxed and they incline toward each other to express their emotional connection. Topics like the weather or other banal things are not necessary between friends; these boring topics are simply silence fillers for strangers to use to avoid talking about emotions.

When you make the decision to be friends with someone you haven't met yet, you are also making the decision to be comfortable with them.

There was a study conducted among Italian adults regarding swearing and likability. Using more informal speech and swear words in political blog posts made voters form better impressions of the political candidates writing the posts. A related study discovered that people found political candidates more relatable and persuasive when they used the word "damn" in a speech about college tuition, as opposed to candidates who avoided using the word.

In a 2017 paper, workers located in the United Kingdom, France, and the United

States used swear words to either get attention or convey urgency, which in turn led to solidarity and friendships. In the workplace, women who swore earned more respect from their male colleagues in male-dominated offices. Yet another study concluded that coworkers who swore more were closer to those they chose to swear around, presumably because of exactly what we have been referencing in this chapter—friendship leads to lowered guards and authentic conversation.

Finally, a study of Swedish workers investigated how they used swearing to convey familiarity and affection to one another. The most popular colleague in the study, an older man named Igor, would reiterate what people said to him but would insert the word "damn," saying things like "Exactly, that is *damn* difficult!"

Based on these studies, you get a clearer picture of the value of treating people as friends. It allows both parties to let loose and be comfortable without the specter of judgment hanging over their heads. If you take the first step, people will relax and understand that you are someone they can also relax around. Of course, this also means the number of conversations you will have about the weather, commuting, and weekend plans will shrink—but that's a good sign that you are discussing realer topics.

Friends talk about personal matters, negative or positive. A study at the State University of New York at Stony Brook, the California Graduate School of Family Psychology, the University of California, Santa Cruz, and Arizona State University showed the power of getting deep and personal. College students were split into pairs and told to spend 45 minutes getting to know each other. They were given questions to ask each other. Only some of the students were told to ask increasingly personal questions. One example of such a question was "What was your relationship with your mother?" Other students only had banal small talk questions, like "How is the weather today?" or "What is your favorite holiday?"

The group who discussed the personal questions reported feeling closer to the other student at the end of the study. Personal details facilitate friendship because that's what friends talk about. It seems circuitous, but the point is that you should even talk about personal things that you would normally shy away from with strangers.

Admittedly, we also don't do this because it's scary. You are quite literally putting yourself out to be rejected and judged when you make such ventures to strangers and acquaintances. This is valid, but the psychological principle known as *reciprocity* will prevent this the vast majority of the time. Reciprocity is where someone tends to pay back and return what they get from you, whether it is positive or negative. For example, if someone buys you lunch, you will feel indebted to them and return their gesture by buying them something or treating them better in some way. In this instance, if you give them such positive energy and openness, people will most likely return it in kind. Psychologically speaking, you don't have much to fear in terms of judgment and rejection.

However, this goes even further with *reciprocity of liking*, another psychological phenomenon that governs our actions. This means that if someone thinks you like him, he is more likely to like you. Since he knows that you like him, he knows that you won't reject him. He also knows that you find something attractive about him, on a friendly level at least, which boosts his ego. You make him feel good so he wants to be around you. He views you as a friendly face and an ally in life if you like him. So when you express friendship to people and make them think that you like them, there are at least two psychological drives that cause us to be accepted and not rejected.

A 1959 study, published in *Human Relations*, found that participants were told that certain members of a group discussion would like them. All of the group members were chosen randomly and did not know each other. The researchers had no idea if they would like each other or not. But after disclosing this, they found that participants best liked the people in the group they were told supposedly liked them back.

More recently, researchers at the University of Waterloo and the University of Manitoba found that when we expect people to accept us, we act warmer toward them. Our warmer behavior makes it more likely that they will like us as a result. So if you don't know how someone feels about you, act like you like them and they will most likely like you back. Again, it's circuitous and reminiscent of questioning whether the chicken or the egg comes first. But it's clear that someone has to act first, so take that role.

The takeaway is that you must decide that someone is your friend, not a stranger, and doing so makes you far more likable. Speak more comfortably, relax your body, lean toward them as they talk, and avoid boring topics with no emotional connection such as the weather. Try to learn about them and find out what you two might have in common. The alternative is a boring conversation that you probably don't want to be part of.

Show Up

Part of making the decision to be friends is making the decision to proactively spend time with people. Friends spend time with friends. Thus, you can't expect a friendship to blossom if you only see them once a month. You need to accept reality and adjust your expectations to match reality. The more face time you spend around someone, the more opportunities you have to expand on your initial efforts at building rapport and closeness. After all, exposure to someone's face breeds the familiarity and comfort that can make people like you, as many studies have shown.

Woody Allen once stated that "eighty percent of success is showing up." Being present just gives you the chance you need to make an impression and forge a close relationship. When you have an opportunity to be around people, take it. Go to parties, stop by a person's desk at work, or go over to someone's house. While social media is a great tool for connecting with people, it does not replace face-to-face interaction. You can use Twitter or Facebook to connect with people and make plans, but be sure it all leads to you being physically present. Actually make the effort and notice the rewards that you reap as a result.

Mere exposure theory is the name of the principle behind this. Mere exposure theory is the phenomenon that people like you the more they see you. People who dislike you will even start to like you more if they are exposed to you enough. While this principle can work with any stimulus, from places to things to products, it works especially well with people. You can think of it as likability and friendship through a passive process, such as osmosis.

Think about when you start a new job. On the first day, some people may rub you the wrong way. They may make poor impressions. You make up your mind that you dislike some of the people in the new workplace. As time passes, however, you start to get used to these people and you even start to befriend them. This is because you see them literally every day and you get used to them. As you become more frequently exposed to people and learn more about them, you start to accept them and even like them.

To be likable, you should maximize the amount of exposures you have with people. The more you see each other, the more you like each other. At some point, however, the linear relationship between exposure and liking starts to wane. This is when you want to think about spending time with people in the form of this simple formula: *frequency + intensity*. You can add more and more intensity to the relationship over time as you speak more profoundly about emotions, fulfill each other's needs, support each other, bond over things in common, and learn how to rely on each other. Suppose you spend time with someone twice a week and always have deep, moving conversations about your differing worldviews. That sounds like a pretty close friend.

Be the Initiator

Given what we have learned about the importance of simply spending time with people, it's important to understand that you must create those opportunities for yourself.

Just like with taking the first step to deciding to be friends, you can't expect other people to create opportunities for you to be more likable. Very few of us are so proactive, and they might even be just as shy and distant around strangers as you are. You have to make the effort and put yourself out there first. Maybe this feels unfair, but it is just how life works. In fact, this is a major sticking point many will have. But imagine Yuval's position as being new in a city and striving to break into existing social circles. It's only natural that he has to be the one making the effort, because the other people involved are all comfortable and settled already.

Most people want to make new friends but lack the courage and willpower to make the first move. They are comfortable with their current friends or have trouble adjusting to the idea that they need to actively welcome people into their lives. They may be afraid of bothering you or of not coming up with something fun to do that you would be interested in joining them in. Finally, they might fear rejection and looking and feeling stupid if you reject the friendship. This is why being new or meeting a new crowd for the first time can make you feel left out. But this hardly means that the whole world is rejecting you.

It's easy to think "If no one invites me out, they must not like me." But maybe they are waiting for you to call them and you are waiting for them to call you. As a result, no one calls anyone. The truth is, everyone is just waiting for others to initiate social connections, not realizing that they should take the first step.

To become more likable, you need to set aside your own shyness and unwillingness to leave your comfort zone. You must make the first move and attempt to get to know people by asking them to go do things with you. If you wait around for others to do this for you, you will be bitterly disappointed. And recall that with the principle of reciprocity of liking, just indicating interest in someone will make them feel more strongly toward you.

Think about how much courage it takes to initiate a friendship. Some people just can't drum up that courage. But since you can, you can continue initiating until your friendship becomes something where you both feel comfortable initiating. Don't overanalyze it when someone fails to initiate. You will hear yes far more often than no. But you will only hear yes if you actually try to make the effort. There are some specific ways to initiate more effectively.

Have a specific plan in place. Being too vague can really make people uncomfortable. You don't ask "Do you want to hang out sometime?" That's too open and still calls for the other person to initiate, so what was the point, exactly? People are lazy and most likely won't follow up other than by agreeing. It also puts them on alert because they don't know what they are potentially agreeing to. Rather, you should step forward with a specific plan in place.

For example, you might say to someone, "Let's hang out," and it will probably never happen because it is so open-ended. But if you say, "I'm having a cookout tonight with four or five of my friends. Want to come by?" that is more specific and the person is more likely to show up. The other person has some guidance and direction and thus feels more comfortable accepting the invitation and actually appearing. You helped them set their expectations for the interaction and prepare.

Additionally, you want to make plans that are attractive to the other person. Find a common activity you both love and then propose that you both go do it. People will be more open to spending time with you if you propose an activity that they will enjoy, at least, so they will have some baseline incentive to go. Keep it simple, specific, and attractive. The same goes for ease—make plans easy for them to attend in terms of commitment, cost, and physical location. All you're doing is increasing your chances that your initiation pays off and you don't initiate something that was only going to be rejected.

Do the first few activities as a group. Sometimes, one-on-one time can be awkward. It can also make it seem like you are trying to get romantic, and others might not be as open to leaving their comfort zones. To get around this, you can propose that you go out with other people and do something as a group. If they ask you who else is coming, you can float some names and ask them "Who else do you think we should invite?" This creates a teamwork ethic where you are both involved in the planning. This is mostly for the benefit of the other person, to increase their level of comfort and ability to open up. Just as big group settings sound daunting to some, small, intimate settings sound intimidating to others.

Get comfortable going out alone. If no one takes you up on your offer and you have no group to go out with, don't feel bad about going by yourself to whatever the intended activity was. Sure, you don't *want* to be the only single person there, but going alone accomplishes at least one of two things. First, it can help with future conversations with these folks. They may ask you, "How was that movie?" You will lose a conversation opportunity if you just reply, "I didn't go." You can also initiate again by adding "Next time you should definitely come."

The other benefit is that you appear less desperate and more confident if you aren't dependent on others to have a good time. People will admire that you still went without them. If you are comfortable being alone in real-world settings, people will be drawn to you because you appear happy and confident.

In addition, if you attend an event solo, you are far more likely to meet new people. If you attend an event with one or two other people, it's par for the course to cluster together the entire time and not meet anyone new. Say you go to a Comic-Con. People tend to like those who they share things in common with, so you can bond with people at these events over shared interests. If you are just hanging out by yourself at home, you will never meet anybody new. After all, who will come knocking on your door, randomly hoping to get to know you?

Join a group. The best way to meet people is to put yourself out there, as we already discussed. But the easiest way to do this is to join some type of group or start a group. In the modern world of social media, finding groups and inviting people you don't even know to go out is easier than ever. You can easily assemble a group or find one. There is a great mobile phone app called Meetup where people with common interests interact and form groups that go out to do things. Finding fun things to do and meeting people with shared interests is incredibly easy with this app. You can also check out Facebook groups for the same purpose.

Overall, instead of getting together and talking about what happened in the past, do something new together so you subsequently will have something to talk about after. People bond over shared experiences and memories, so make memories with people, even those you barely know. This applies to old friendships as well. Yes, you have to initiate and keep working at old friendships, too. They can decay with time and boredom if no one makes effort, and often you will be the one who has to make the effort if you want to see any change. Remember, no one is obligated to make the first move and most people won't anyway because it is too hard, so to see results, you must make the effort yourself.

Takeaways:

- A highly underrated facet of being likable is the simple decision to treat people like friends instead of like strangers. It sounds small, but it affects everything you say or do toward people. This chapter is about making that conscious choice and realizing that you aren't doing it.

- When you make the decision, you might also realize how passive you generally are in regards to seeking out new people. This might be because of fear of judgment and rejection. But rejection and judgment are far away due to reciprocity and reciprocity of liking. The mere exposure effect also helps, as there is a clear linear relationship between time spent with someone and overall affection for them.

- Therefore, we must usually be the first person to spring into action, because others aren't conditioned to, which leads to a stalemate of each party waiting for the other to act first. You have to take initiative and be the initiator and planner, at least at first. Be specific with your plan, make it easy for them, and be comfortable going out without others.

Chapter 2: The Principle of Self-Disclosure

Sharon is the type of person who *overshares*. Her family and friends hate this and tell her not to do it, but she does it anyway as it is just part of who she is. As a result, Sharon will strike up a conversation with literally anyone and will talk about anything—her sex life, her childhood, her relationship with her mom, her likes and dislikes, and her political views. She has a huge diversity of friends from all over who enjoy talking to her. They know a lot about her, but she also knows a lot about them. Her ability to throw modesty to the wind and talk freely about herself attracts people to her.

Ellen liked Sharon for this very reason. Yet Ellen hates self-disclosure and tries to get Sharon to stop it. When Ellen meets new people, she doesn't share much about herself and refuses to disclose personal details about her life. It takes her a long time to open up to anyone. Therefore, she is mysterious and people don't know how to read her. They tend to like her well enough because she comes across as nice and harmless, but they don't get close to her because they see no reason to. She has far fewer friends than Sharon does. Perhaps if she were more like Sharon and more open about herself, she might have better luck pulling in new friends.

Sharing more about yourself can make others like you more. The principle of self-disclosure involves disclosing information about yourself to make people more interested and emotionally invested in you. It can also make people feel closer to you and more open to sharing things about themselves in exchange. Sharing things about yourself works because it makes you become a real three-dimensional human they can relate to and feel familiar with. When you self-disclose, others will, too, and that's where you really start to break through barriers.

The problem is, most people don't do this off the bat. Like in the first principle, you must make the first move and start disclosing things about yourself to encourage the other person to do so. Sadly, the responsibility to initiate likability again falls on you.

Sharing More

Now you may wonder just what to share. What kind of information should you impart? What information is TMI (too much information) and hence will make people not like you? What information is beneficial to share with others and enhances your likability? What should you keep private?

Generally, the more you disclose, the better. TMI is beneficial for your likability because, again, this is how friends relate. Friends are notorious for oversharing without shame or inhibition. They may laugh, gag, or declare "I didn't need to know that!" But they still share everything. So even if you feel that you are entering TMI territory, that is still better than not disclosing anything because you are still treating others like your friends. This ties into the first principle that we have already discovered and allows you to kill two birds with one stone. By undersharing, you present a version of yourself who is afraid to make any waves and is ultimately very forgettable.

Share what is on your mind. TMI might include details of your sex life or your controversial opinions. In polite conversation with strangers, these details are not appropriate. But friends love to cross polite boundaries, so to put both this principle and the first one into play, overshare on things you normally would not share with strangers to gain more leverage and likability with others. Share slowly at first to gauge people's responses, but once you get the sense that someone is on the same page and willing to befriend you as well, you can open the floodgates, so to speak.

The more you reveal about yourself, the more connection points you generate with the other person. You reveal things you like or dislike, which the other person may be able to relate to and disagree or agree with. You can find more things in common as you reveal your preferences, opinions, loves, hates, likes, dislikes, sensitivities, memories, emotions, thoughts, and anecdotes.

For example, say you are at a party and meeting with people you have never seen before. Usually this situation is daunting and you feel awkward and clam up with a drink in your hand to protect your fragile ego from rejection by these new people. But using the tips in this book, you disclose a lot about yourself and you talk about how much you like fishing, anime, and knitting, all three of your seemingly unrelated hobbies. You have stories about each of these that you can launch into from normal small talk questions. They speak to your interests, how you react to situations, and your personality in general.

Everyone in the room who loves one of those three things (or can simply relate to how you might react to a situation) can now connect with you, and a conversation is born based on the topic you two share. All you needed to do was answer questions with a series of details about yourself or tell a story about yourself.

This about it this way: provide three details where you would have replied with a one-word answer, or provide three sentences where you would have replied with one sentence. That's the basic type of step that is needed for self-disclosure to work its wonders. If you had a boring weekend, still name three details so people aren't left with nothing to work with. It might feel extraneous at first, but it might also let you realize how little you disclose about yourself to others.

Share your emotions. The reason emotions are so powerful is because they are universal. Everyone in the world, from Americans to Aboriginals to African bush people, share similar emotions, emotional responses, and even facial expressions. Scientific studies have shown that people from different cultures can recognize what smiles and frowns mean, which indicates that all people feel and express emotions in similar ways. So expressing your emotions and making them known to others is a foolproof method to get others to feel close to you. You become more human and relatable when you express your emotions. Others feel more comfortable expressing their own emotions and agreeing or disagreeing with how you feel once you dare to be open about your emotions. Again, this starts with talking about how happy or sad something makes you—that's all it takes to open a deeper dialogue.

Share stories from your own life. Again, this makes you seem more real and three-dimensional. Even though it doesn't feel like it, we all go through similar circumstances and struggles every day. We all brush our teeth, hate waking up, and commute to some kind of job. You have some part of your life story that others can relate to. This makes people feel closer to you and lets them laugh and talk about how they went through the same thing. Often, they will start to tell their stories based on yours.

We all have common experiences. We all remember when we learned to ride a bike, embarrassing moments in high school, or disasters in dating. Share your story with gusto to make it seem more engaging and entertaining. Finally, give people room to interject with their own stories so that they can feel as if they are participating and relating to you. You won't be as likable if you hog the spotlight and never let others talk. The purpose of sharing is to encourage mutual sharing, so don't keep things focused on you.

Ultimately, you want to just get into the habit of talking about yourself more and sharing things you wouldn't necessarily think about sharing right now. You can work on even just thinking out loud more. You seem more real to others and you ensure that others can relate to you. You create more conversations out of thin air.

It can be intimidating. You have been taught your whole life to be modest and even private. Now you are going against years of teachings. You may worry that you are bothering others or overstepping boundaries. But the thing is, you will find that people actually love it when you talk about yourself more and become more open. You will have an easier time capturing others' attention, forming bonds, and even having fun with others just because you talk about yourself more.

No Judging

If you are still on the fence about opening up about yourself, here are some scientific studies that support the veracity of this.

A 1989 study by Hilton and Fein set out to determine the cause of people's judgments, assumptions, and stereotyping. What made the brain immediately assign traits and a veritable backstory to some people versus others? Why were some people so quick to jump to conclusions?

It was found that the less information people had about a certain subject or person, the more they began to fill in the gaps with information that was stereotypical of a general representation. If I described someone who belonged to a country club, drove an expensive car, played tennis, and liked lacrosse, there's a very specific image you might conjure up.

To prevent stereotyping and being instantly judged, Hilton and Fein found that simply providing details about the subject completely unrelated to the stereotype in mind diluted the stereotype and made people more likely to trust and like others. The more detail about the person, the better, even if it was completely random. When we have limited information, we assume a person is just the same as the most stereotypical representation that has those traits.

When we have more information about someone in any regard, we realize we can't define them by those one or two traits, and we cease stereotyping and judging. You can make people like you more, stereotype you less, and emotionally invest in you more by providing seemingly useless and nonsensical details about your life. People like to make fun of TMI, but the reality is that TMI can ultimately make you more likable. Of course, preferably you share positive or at least neutral information about yourself.

You become less of a threat and more of a known quantity. People become less suspicious of you and are more willing to give you the benefit of the doubt. By sharing seemingly trivial information about yourself, you allow people to feel like they know you, and they stop making assumptions.

And again, it doesn't even matter if the details are relevant to your identity, career, nonthreatening nature, or life. You can share your preference of glasses brand, your favorite color, and perhaps where you went to school. The more information about you that is out there, the less readily people can judge and stereotype you, simply because you won't fit those stereotypes and assumptions anymore.

For example, what if we learned that the person who plays tennis and belongs to a country club was poor growing up and went to college on a tennis scholarship? Also, they drive a 20-year-old car and prefer to eat burritos. Does that change your view of them? We certainly wouldn't stereotype and make more assumptions about them like we previously did. In fact, the additional information we've learned blows the doors off any category we could put them into. And in a sense, that's the goal: to make it impossible for us to fit into any broad category or generalization. People are only judging you based on what they *aren't* seeing of you.

With more information, people suddenly become three-dimensional and not the static character biographies we see in movies. We are humanized, and we eventually realize that all humans are complex amalgamations. We were never going to fit into a stereotype or box. In reality, you really haven't done anything profound. You haven't even given any information that's important or useful.

Oversharing to maximize likability works to get people to feel that they know different sides of you. An easy way to share more details is to get into the habit of offering unsolicited information. For instance, if someone asks about your weekend, don't resort to answering, "Good, how about yours?" A guideline I like to use is to give four distinct details when answering easy questions—in this way, you will get into the habit of giving people more information, which will make conversation flow better anyway. Here's an example of zero sharing, little information, and a high likelihood of judgment and stereotyping.

Where are you from?
Oklahoma. You?

If you don't know anything about a person besides the fact they are from Oklahoma, where does your mind automatically go? It goes to whatever your stereotypes about Oklahoma are. You don't know if this person was born there, raised there, or only lived there for a couple of years. You don't have the context to make a good judgment about them, and yet you do anyway. This one trait defines them in your mind.

Now, here's an example of why giving unsolicited information can be helpful.

Where are you from?
Oklahoma, but I was born in New York. My parents were originally from France and I grew up visiting France very frequently. Also, I have eight dogs.

Now attempt to put *this* person into a box. It's the same person as before, but it's nearly impossible because there is so much information about them that you simply have to take them as they are. By knowing more about them, they have become more humanized and interesting.

The added benefit to sharing unsolicited information and more in general is you make it extremely easy for others to connect with you. When you spout off details about your life, it's easy for them to find common ground and know you as a person. If you divulge personal information or intimate details of your life, you'll also be appearing to take the first steps to building trust and showing vulnerability to others. The more that's out there, the more there is for people to hook on to and relate to.

In 1997, Arthur Aron found that sharing did more than simply make you less susceptible to judgment from others. It creates emotional closeness and investment. In fact, the more intimate and *invasive* the information, the better.

He split participants into two groups. One group questioned each other on 36 very specific and intimate questions, including personal vulnerabilities and insecurities. Sample questions were "What is your most terrible memory?" and "What is your most treasured memory?" It's impossible to not get personal when faced with these questions. The other group was tasked to ask each other only shallow small talk questions about their everyday lives.

It's not something people are comfortable doing, but the participants followed directions. We feel like we're offending people or showing too much of ourselves, which is frightening. But the participants who were tasked with asking each other sensitive and sometimes prying personal questions developed greater levels of trust, rapport, and mutual comfort with one another. They felt emotional closeness, even though they didn't know each other before the study. Here are some examples of the questions used:

1. Do you want to be famous? For what?

This tells you what a person really values or imagines themselves to be skilled at. This can reveal someone's deepest desires and fantasies.

2. If you were able to live up to 90 and save either the mind or body of a 30-year-old, which thing would you want to save?

You learn whether someone values the physical or mental more. You also learn if someone is honest or not.

3. If you could change anything about how you were raised, what would you change?

Here you gain deep insight into someone's past and history. You learn about his or her regrets and if his or her childhood was happy. You may learn some deeply personal secrets about someone.

4. If you could wake up tomorrow with any one quality, what would that quality be?

This question enables you to learn what someone wants to be and what he or she values in a person. The person you are asking this question of will always answer with the quality that matters most to him or her.

5. Is there something that you have wanted to do for a long time? Why haven't you done it yet?

People all have dreams. They also have regrets. Asking someone this lets you uncover what he or she dreams of or what he or she regrets not doing. It also makes him or her like you more because you are essentially goading this person to live his or her dream before it's too late.

The other group, however, didn't develop this level of trust, confidence, and intimacy. They essentially remained at their initial level of emotional closeness. Aron proved that when *you* share information, the *receiving parties* will like you more and feel closer to you and reciprocate.

Finally, according to a study by Theodore Newcomb, people tend to like those who are similar to them. The *similarity-attraction effect* is where people are drawn to like people. Newcomb measured his subjects' views on things like sex and politics and then sorted them into a house to live together. The subjects who shared the same viewpoints were usually friendlier by the end of the study than those with dissimilar viewpoints.

To compound the results of Newcomb's study, another study conducted by researchers at the University of Virginia and Washington University in St. Louis found that Air Force recruits tended to get along better with those who shared their negative personality traits rather than their positive ones. But here's the thing. You can only discover similarities when you self-disclose. So by sharing more about yourself, you can find things in common that make others like you more.

Getting Others to Disclose

When you self-disclose, others will usually reciprocate. But sometimes they do not. In fact, some people are like talking to brick walls. How can you get others to self-disclose more consistently so it isn't one-sided sharing?

There are some basic, tried-and-true ways. You can ask questions such as "How do you feel about this weather?" instead of asking yes or no questions, as these will just get you monosyllabic answers. Instead, engage people by asking in-depth questions that provoke them to think and come up with a detailed response. There might seem to be little difference, but one version asks about emotions and can conjure up memories about the weather. Ask better questions and get better answers.

You can also appeal to their interests. People love to chat about what they enjoy doing. Ask a person about his favorite hobbies and request that he teach you about it. Ask someone about his job as a flight attendant and how flying all of the time feels. You will get a person to open up if you try to talk about things they care about or like. Everyone has a narrative to their life—stories that sum up how they ended up where they are. Ask about their stories and they will be more than glad to document the twists and turns.

Finally, you can stroke someone's ego. This will make him or her feel good and want to open up to get even more positive ego stroking. So you might tell a person, "I find your career fascinating. Tell me all about it!" Or you might say, "You have the most gorgeous garden. How do you get your crocuses to bloom so late in the year?" Prompt them to speak by first building them up with a compliment.

You can't control what others do, but you can choose to be the first to disclose. The law of reciprocation may just work for you. But is there a way to do this slightly more organically? There is a fancy term called *elicitation* that makes it easier to get others to disclose. Elicitation is a type of questioning that uses a conversational style to disguise how you are sneakily obtaining information from someone.

To use elicitation, you make a statement that plays on the other person's desire to respond for a variety of reasons. The other person will feel driven to respond in a certain way, even if they had no prior interest in engaging. The FBI came up with this term and often uses it in interrogation to get confessions or answers from people. A direct question may not always get a direct answer; thus, it becomes important to phrase things differently to obtain information.

Here is an example of how elicitation works, as provided by the FBI. You are trying to plan a surprise party for someone, so you need to know his schedule, his friends' contact information, and his food and drink preferences. Of course, you can't ask him for this information directly. So how might you discover these pieces of information from him?

You might make a presumptive statement: "I'm going to buy a grape soda. Do you want one?" This will seem like a random, harmless question and he will correct you: "No, I prefer root beer." Now you know his drink preferences. Then you can ask, "What time are you off work every night? My friend is looking for someone to help move." He will tell you his work schedule as a result. And so, you've gained valuable information without having directly asked for it.

What's important is that elicitation is meant to break the dam and get people to start engaging and talking. There are various types of elicitation techniques according to researcher Ellen Naylor, and some of them are documented below.

Recognition. People thrive when you recognize something good about them. Mention "I love your sweater," and you will get a story about how the wearer obtained the sweater. Mention "You are very thorough" and you will get a story about how the person went to military school and learned to be thorough at all times. They may have been tight-lipped before, but any chance to enhance praise is welcome. People have a natural desire to feel recognized and appreciated, so give them an opening to show off a little.

You can also show appreciation to someone and compliment them. This is similar to recognition; people rarely turn down an opportunity to explain their accomplishments.

Complaining. People love to complain, so you can get a person to commiserate with you by complaining first. If they don't commiserate, they might open up the other way by feeling compelled to defend what you are complaining about. Either way, you've opened them up and gotten some information out of them.

You might tell someone at work, "I hate these long hours without overtime pay," and he will go into more detail about how he needs money from not being paid enough. This may lead him to disclose more about his home life and how many kids he has and marital issues he has related to finances. It may also lead to him disclosing how he deals with money problems. Either way, you have more information now.

Key to this technique is creating a safe environment for people to brag, complain, or show other raw emotion. If you complain first, they feel that no negative topics are taboo, which creates a judgment-free zone. They don't feel like they will get in trouble with you. You don't have to complain to kickstart this; just express your own negative emotions, vulnerabilities, or disappointments. People will figure "Hey, if they talked about something so personal that casts them in a negative light, I guess I can talk about anything here."

Correction. People love to be right. So if you say something wrong, they will gladly jump at the chance to correct you. This leads back to the earlier example about using presumptive statements to find out how to plan a surprise birthday party. If you give people an opportunity to flex their ego, most will seize it happily.

An easy way to do this is to state something you know to be obviously incorrect to see if they will step in and break their silence. You can also state your assumptions about a person or situation and see if they agree or disagree. "Yeah, I figured you for a vegetarian. You look like you don't like meat."

Self-effacement. People have a tendency to downplay their achievements and appear modest. Find out what someone is proud of and then ask him about it. He will downplay it with a blush. So then prompt him to tell you more or tell him that he obviously accomplished something huge, and he will want to elaborate, either to further be modest or to brag a bit about his deeds. For example, ask him about his great golf victories if you notice golf trophies on his desk. Say, "You must be a golf champion!" and he will say no and then start to brag about his victories.

Naïveté. To be clear, this does not mean to act stupid; it means to act like you're on the cusp of understanding. Acting naïve makes people feel compelled to teach, instruct, and show off their knowledge. People just can't resist enlightening you, especially if you're 95% of the way there and all people have to do is figuratively finish your sentence. "I understand most of this theory, but there's just this one thing I'm unclear on. It could mean so many things..."

Shift the window. This is where you say something slightly outrageous that you know won't be answered, then pretend like you didn't bring it up. Why does this work? Does it even work? It's because you have put something out there to dramatically change the tone of the conversation but then taken it back to not be addressed.

Think of it as a cumulative effect—when you do this a couple of times, these are the types of questions people will engage with and answer even if they were ice cold beforehand. You haven't actually committed a faux pas per se, but you've shifted the boundaries of the conversation. It's a good combination that can get people to lower their guards without them even realizing it, and eventually their window of what they feel is appropriate to be shared can shift and widen.

Sometimes if you make your initial statement here outrageous and provocative enough, you might bait them into responding regardless. The more provocative, the better, if you are really having trouble getting a peep from someone.

Silence. Give people space to speak. When you take a step back, people will feel compelled to take a step forward and break the awkward tension. If you signal that you expect someone to speak and are waiting for them, they may open their mouths to meet your expectation.

Takeaways:

- The principle of self-disclosure is a surprising one because it makes most people uncomfortable at first. But realizing that TMI is a powerful weapon in finding connection points with people can push most through the zone of discomfort. The truth is, sharing more about your emotions, life stories, and experiences will help you connect with people because they are universal. Plus, sharing more makes people judge and stereotype you less.

- When you disclose more, you are able to find similarities more easily with people, and similarity is a precursor to comfort, which is a precursor to likability. Of course, you want to share relatively slowly at first so you can gauge people's response.
- We know we should disclose more, and once we get into the habit, it's not that difficult. But what about compelling other people to reciprocate, which they may or may not always do? Sure, you can talk about their interests, stroke their ego, or ask better questions, but a better method is to use elicitation. Elicitation is using indirect phrasing to make people feel like they need to speak up at that very moment.
- Types of elicitation include recognition and praise, complaining and sharing of negative emotions, making people correct you, self-effacement, naïveté, shifting the window, provocative statements, and silence.

Chapter 3: The Principle of Safety and Comfort

My friend Steve used to have a lot of trouble when meeting new people. Frankly, most were turned off by him because he tended to see matters in only black and white. He would see something that didn't comply with his narrow view of the world and be very vocal about it. He was judging people right in front of their faces and expecting them to see the light of his logic and suddenly agree with him. Needless to say, that was never going to end well, and it wasn't until a physical altercation after a comment about someone's shoes that he realized that he needed to change his ways.

Steve was a jerk, but what was he actually doing to people? He was making them feel unsafe and uncomfortable—like they couldn't let their guards down around him lest they be judged.

This principle is about making people feel comfortable and safe with you. Liking arises only when feelings of familiarity and comfort are present, and you can kickstart the process of being liked by focusing on building feelings of trust, reliability, and overall safety. Steve made sure that people's guards and defenses were always up, so we want to create the opposite effect. People just need to feel like they can be themselves around you.

The lowest hanging fruit for us to start with is feelings of negativity and how to cope with them.

Negative Emotion Management

We all feel negative emotions. The difference between someone who is likable and someone who is not is how we deal with these emotions. Whatever the circumstances, if you are outwardly angry, sullen, or irritable, people will avoid you in the fear that you will be their next target. That's the feeling of lack of safety. People won't feel comfortable being themselves around you if you are constantly upset, overly critical, hateful, or volatile.

This isn't about hiding your emotions necessarily, or even faking them, but if our goal is making people feel comfortable around us, you can't be a ticking time bomb that people won't feel comfortable around because they don't know when you will blow up. It's like being around someone throwing a tantrum or not handling conflict well. You have to manage your negative emotions in a way where you can still express yourself but not send people running for shelter. People have to know that whatever happens to stays with you, and you won't punish others for something they were not involved in.

First, be nice whenever negativity occurs. Sounds simple enough. The situation is likely tense enough that you shouldn't be making it worse by injecting your emotions into it.

When someone is wrong, don't rub it in his or her face. It is unnecessary and only serves your ego. Making someone feel wrong in front of people causes unnecessary tension and strife. The person you humiliate will forever resent you. In the same vein, avoid criticizing someone too much and acting like you are better than them or pointing out their flaws or mistakes around others. Criticism hits hard, so you should use only the bare minimum to make your point understood.

When you are right and someone else is wrong, give that individual a face-saving way to carry out your wishes with a minimum of embarrassment and humiliation. Instead of asserting your right to be right, ask people for their advice on the next steps to rectify mistakes. That allows them to be part of the decision-making process and not just the butt of a joke. Make them feel safe to be wrong and show flaws around you.

When it comes to you being in the wrong, it has the potential to go just as badly. This typically happens when you become defensive when receiving criticism. This is your ego and sense of pride at work. Try to be gracious about it, apologize if necessary, and listen rather than defend. Again, you want to make people feel safe in bringing you their unfiltered thoughts, even if that paints you in a negative light.

Don't take out your negative feelings like anger, jealousy, sullenness, or resentment on others. Feel them and express them, but the difference is that you shouldn't allow them to affect how you interact with others in any way. You want to minimize the negative emotions you project because your feelings are not anyone else's problem. If you are in a poor mood, don't act in a way to put others into the same mood.

The easiest way to minimize these feelings is to divert them. Let go of thoughts that hurt you, because when you think negative thoughts, you can't help but fixate and you lower your own mood. If even for a second, your feelings flash across your face, even if you don't intend for them to. So limit the bad thinking and think more positive thoughts. Focus on what is good in life and what you are grateful for. Everyone faces hardships in life, yet some people are still lovable and a joy to be around when they are at their lowest moments.

This is because they can manage their negative emotions effectively and even productively. To harp on the same theme, you want to impart feelings of safety that people can be negative with you. If we can assume that 50% of the world's topics are negative by nature, this opens up a whole range of topics and emotions that people can explore with you.

Again, of course bad events will have a negative effect on you. It is naïve to assume that you won't ever be hurt or disturbed by the bad things that can happen in life. Feel your emotions and express them, but don't have them affect your interactions or take your emotions out on others. You will creep people out if you have no normal reactions to life. For example, if you were to lose your job, you want to act sad and let your grief or horror show.

Negative emotion management makes people feel safe around you and feel confident that you aren't going to attack. It makes you predictable in a good way—where people know they can expect only positivity from you and that you are someone they can turn to for support and cheer. In this way, you can become more reliable and dependable for people, and that's always quite likable.

Appear Transparent

Transparency is the quality where you appear like you are not hiding anything. Honest and trustworthy is the impression you want to give. You want to appear as if you are who you say you are, with no ulterior motives lurking beneath your smile. This can be hard to do even if you don't have anything to hide.

The first way to accomplish this is to speak in a straightforward manner. This isn't about your enunciation or clarity of speech; it's about how forthcoming you are with information.

When people ask you questions, answer directly and provide information freely. Being evasive suggests that you are hiding something, but coming out with the truth makes you appear totally honest. Information is funny in that when you present it to people, they care far less about it. In other words, people don't care about your secrets or private information unless they sense you are trying to keep it hidden. Thus, keep a clean track record of being forthcoming and people will trust you more and more.

Another way to be transparent is to emphasize equity in relationships. This means making sure that there is equality in all areas of a relationship; this doesn't just refer to one party continually treating the other to lunch. Treat others as you would want to be treated. Insist on paying back all debts and get the message across that you're not using people or looking to take advantage of them. This makes it extremely clear that you're not seeking to gain at the expense of others.

You want to always be consistent in your actions and words. Don't be one person to Bob and then someone completely different to John. It is the very definition of two-faced. Don't make people wonder what lie you're telling them; make them feel that they know the real you instead of one of your many masks. It is very disconcerting to hear that someone told you they loved fish, while you heard from someone else that they hated fish. It seems like something so insignificant, but it calls into doubt how truthful they are in general.

Don't Be Judgmental

Humans are naturally judgmental. You look at someone and you immediately form an idea about who that person is and whether or not you like that person. When someone does something, you automatically form an opinion. But being judgmental only pushes people away, at least if you express your judgment. Even if you're just judging others in front of people, who knows when you'll turn your sights onto them for judgment! Rather than pushing people away, be open-minded with the Japanese concept of *wabi sabi.*

While this term has no direct translation from Japanese into English, it's a term for what makes people who they are. *Wabi* is the quirks and glitches that people possess that separate them from everyone else. For example, someone might never match their socks. That is a unique personality identifier because it is an anomaly. *Sabi* is the inherent beauty of an individual that grows with life experience. Think of how beautiful an old man is as he shares a plethora of stories from a time way before you were born, gracing you with knowledge that you never previously had about that era of history. Therefore, together, wabi sabi is about enjoying and cherishing imperfections.

The roots of wabi sabi can be traced to ancient Buddhist teachings, where embracing imperfection is seen as the first step to achieving enlightenment, or *satori*. Seeing into yourself and into others and just accepting what you see without trying to change it is the ultimate form of enlightenment. It's also a good way to become likable.

An example of using this concept in real life might be trying to get to know a homeless man's story and trying to empathize with him instead of judging him for being dirty and assuming that he is on the streets by his own fault. Or it might be accepting it when your friend makes a silly decision and being there for your friend through the fallout, rather than judging your friend and expressing your disappointment. See a flaw or unwise decision you might judge and understand instead that it is a facet of wabi sabi and people are just trying their best each day.

After all, an Austrian robotics study called "To Err Is Robot: How Humans Assess and Act Toward an Erroneous Social Robot" found that people related more to robots that have their own unique flaws and quirks, rather than perfect robots without flaws. It illustrates how quirks define and make up one's personality, making a person relatable and ultimately likable. Getting to know and accepting one's quirks makes you get along with the person better. No human is perfect, so learn to embrace their imperfections as part of what makes them unique. For that matter, what's *your* wabi sabi?

Thus, the flaws you might judge people on make them more likable than a hypothetical perfect version. Imperfection and freedom from judgment make people feel more comfortable around you because they feel allowed to be imperfect. They are more open to expressing themselves. While we should accept this in others, we must also strive to accept it in ourselves, which is what the next point discusses.

Instead of being perfect and inaccessible to others, you want to be a vulnerable human. This makes you more likable because you don't intimidate others. Other people can find that more relatable and will feel more comfortable around you as a result.

To be vulnerable is to admit your flaws. Don't pretend to be perfect. Just admit and even embrace your flaws without apology. This shows both confidence and your authenticity as a person. The previous point was about not judging people on their flaws to be likable, and here, if you don't judge your own flaws harshly, you are more likable. Showing vulnerability and the ability to laugh at yourself also makes you predictable in a comforting way.

In the Pratfall effect, competent individuals committed a blunder or goof and then onlookers perceived them to be more likable and relatable. Imagine if you have a perfect boss, for example. You might not feel comfortable being yourself around him and thus you don't like him as much. But when this boss goofs by spilling coffee on himself, you suddenly feel more comfortable because you realize that he is only human, too. You also feel less restricted in your own actions and less pressure to be perfect.

Finally, show your real emotions and don't keep a perpetual poker face. There has been research that indicates how people will like you more if you express your emotions as opposed to being emotionless.

A 2016 study in Oregon videotaped people watching a fake orgasm scene (funny) in *When Harry Met Sally* and an emotional scene (sad) in *The Champ.* One set of participants were instructed to watch these scenes without showing their emotions, while the other set was told to be as emotional as possible. Those who showed more emotion were generally rated more likable. According to the researchers, "People... do not pursue close relationships indiscriminately—they probably look for people who are likely to reciprocate their investments. So when perceivers detect that someone is hiding their emotions, they may interpret that as a disinterest in the things that emotional expression facilitates— closeness, social support, and interpersonal coordination." Showing real emotions is the epitome of being vulnerable, and there is real evidence that it is more likable than the alternative. Showing emotions is also the epitome of being transparent with others.

Make Someone's Day

To be a truly likable in terms of safety and comfort, you must make people feel good. People must associate you with happiness and positivity. Thankfully, this is easier to achieve than you might think.

It doesn't necessarily require taking the time to go out of your way. Just strive to leave someone in a better condition than when you found them. After every interaction, ask yourself "Did I leave this person in a better condition than I found him or her? Did I uplift, inspire, and empower him or her? Did I cheer him up? Did I make him or her laugh? Did I give some love and support?"

If you approach social interactions with this simple intention, you will always know what to do and how to create feelings of trust and comfort. You will become very likable because you actually make an effort to make others happy, and this will make others associate you with feeling good. They will want to spend more time around you since you are a genuinely caring and nice person who reaches out.

A good example may be to cheer up a person who looks sad. Maybe your coworker comes in looking like she had a really rough day before her shift. Ask her what's wrong and try to comfort her. Bring her favorite lunch, just to get a smile out of her. You might be the only person who takes any action to make her feel better. She will notice this, and she will appreciate it.

Remember, all you wanted to do was leave this person in a better condition than before your interaction. This can be as easy as making them smile or laugh, but the point is, it's completely focused on them. That's appropriate, because likability is not about you or what you gain from an interaction. If you keep in mind this intention of making people's day, it becomes crystal clear how to act to be more likable as a human being.

Takeaways:

- This chapter is focused on being predictable—in a good way. When you're predictable in a good way, it means people feel comfortable around you and aren't worried that you are going to throw a temper tantrum on them. It allows people to feel okay with letting their guards down.
- The first way to create a safe and comforting presence is to learn negative emotion management. This is where you learn to deal with negativity, criticism, being wrong, and not taking things out on other people.
- Being transparent is another way to make people feel safe. When you're

transparent, people don't feel like you're hiding something or using them for some nefarious purpose. You can create this feeling when you're relatively free with information, not evasive, and consistent with how you present yourself to different people.

- Don't be judgmental. Everyone has flaws, which is a concept repeated by the Japanese theory of wabi sabi; imperfection is the very thing that makes something beautiful and unique. Furthermore, vulnerability has been shown to be likable and charming as seen by the Pratfall effect.
- Overall, just make someone's day and be intentional about it. You probably don't think this way because you're thinking about yourself most of the time, but taking in this mindset makes it extremely clear how to be more likable for others.

Chapter 4: The Principle of Listening

One of my former friends Crystal is a *horrible* listener. I would say something and she would behave as if she hadn't heard a word. She was always interrupting me or failing to acknowledge what I had said before saying what she had to say. Needless to say, I started hating talking to her. I found our conversations irritating because I felt as if there was no point in speaking. After a few of these grating conversations, I started to avoid her. I can't say I remember the last time we spoke.

That's around when I met my friend Tammy. Tammy made talking fun and easy. I did not actually realize why our talks were so fun at first, but with some analysis, I realized that it was because she was actually listening and responding to me. She heard what I said instead of ignoring me to think of what she wanted to say next. She would nod her head and respond as I talked. Then she would respond when I finished.

The difference between these two people lies in their listening skills. To be more likable, you must listen hard and listen well. Listening well will make others feel important, respected, and validated. In turn, they will enjoy talking to you more because they feel as if you care.

There are a few simple ways that you can improve your listening skills. As a general matter, listening is not a passive activity. It's not just the act of silence and waiting. People need to know and feel that you are processing what they are saying. They also need to feel that your response is coming from somewhere thoughtful.

Responsiveness

How you respond to someone is a huge part of listening. Being responsive means that you answer their questions and give them feedback. You respond to what they say emotionally, showing that you are involved in the conversation and receiving their messages to the fullest extent.

Karen Huang and her colleagues from Harvard University found that there are three main components to being responsive. Following these steps helps you be a better listener.

The first component is to be understanding. This is when you get an accurate understanding and perception of what the other person is expressing and their feelings. You can do this literally by saying something like "I bet that's hard" as your friend details her recent break-up. You want people to know you are capable of putting yourself in their shoes and knowing the emotions that are flying about at the moment.

The next component is to be validating. You want to respect the other person's viewpoint. So when you are having a political discussion with someone, you might disagree, but you should still say, "I understand why you think that and I respect your opinion. But here is my opinion and why I disagree. I'm not saying you're wrong. I just see it from a different perspective." Validating is the feeling that someone is justified in their thoughts and is understood. You don't necessarily have to be agreed with, but heard and felt to be reasonable and respected.

The final component is to be caring. This is where you express affection and concern. A good example is hugging your friend as she talks about breaking up with her boyfriend. Another example is asking "Are you okay?" when someone is talking has a run of bad luck or an upsetting ordeal. What can we do with this knowledge of optimal responsiveness?

According to Huang, one conversational technique that covers all three components of responsiveness is *question-asking*. We can make guesses about other people's feelings, but the only way to really understand is to ask. Further, the very act of asking questions implies validation for the other's points of view. And especially when we ask follow-up questions, we demonstrate that we truly care about a partner. We are responding in a way that truly shows our concern and authenticity.

As expected, the people who asked lots of questions were rated as *more likable* than those who asked fewer questions. The researchers speculated that this was because the respondents interpreted question-asking as responsiveness. In the end, we all like talking about ourselves, and conversation partners who ask lots of questions fulfill our need to self-disclose. Ironically, those who were asked lots of questions knew *less* about their partners but still liked them more. There's a valuable lesson here that is key to likability in general, and it's going to be repeated throughout this book: make it about other people and you are on the right path.

This also echoes one of Dale Carnegie's more famous quotes from his seminal book *How to Win Friends and Influence People:* "You can make more friends in two months by becoming interested in other people than you can in two years by trying to get other people interested in you."

Monitor

Another purpose of better listening is that you can monitor them to gain self-awareness. Other people are really a mirror for yourself because you can look at them and see how you are faring, if they like you, how well you are speaking, and how you should calibrate your behavior to get better reactions. In other words, monitor their reactions and you can see yourself and how you are doing.

This helps you figure out if you should keep talking about something, if you are angering someone, or if you have touched a nerve. You can monitor your conversation and adjust it to please someone and become more likable as a result if you pay attention to feedback. Listening is not all about hearing words—it's also about monitoring other things, like body language and facial expressions, to gain valuable feedback about the other person's feelings.

As you talk with someone, really observe him or her. Read him or her for signs that you should talk more, talk less, or stop talking altogether. You want to make sure this person doesn't appear uncomfortable. You can do this by reading the feedback this person gives you. Feedback is everywhere. Watch if they flush or tense up or relax. Watch if they seem jittery and nervous or relaxed and at ease. Watch if their smile slips, if they start to frown, or if they start to laugh. Also observe how they act around others and compare it to how they act toward you. For example, a girl who is laughing and relaxed with her friends and the waitstaff but tense and weird when she talks to you is probably uncomfortable. You should adjust your approach to help her relax and like you more.

Pay attention to how a person changes from what you would consider baseline normal behavior given the circumstances. For instance, someone should be relaxed at a brunch with friends. Do their behavior or reactions differ when they speak to you? How so? This allows you to more effectively use other people as tools to monitor yourself.

Monitoring by definition means you are focusing your attention on the other person and looking outward rather than inward toward yourself. The theme of thinking first of others is a theme that runs deep. When you are listening, don't be formulating responses in your head and planning what you will say next—that just means a lack of listening and monitoring for valuable signals. Just listen and then respond, even if you need a couple of seconds to formulate the response. Pay attention to the words they use and the details they cite. Observe their behavior, body language, and facial expressions.

All the information you need about yourself is right in front of you, reflected in the other person.

Validate

One of the main purposes of listening is to validate. When you validate someone in listening, you don't need to agree with them, but you let them know that they are heard. Whatever the sentiment is, it is respected and it matters. Whatever emotion they are feeling, it is justified and its impact is to be fully felt by all. **Validation is, in essence, the act of helping someone feel heard and understood.** It has the power to calm fears and concerns, add a boost to joy and excitement, avoid or quickly resolve arguments, make people much more open to your advice, and *much more.*

Imagine you tell a story about the most fun you've ever had skiing with your sister.

Whoever you are talking to seems pleasant enough, they listen intently, and they reply something like, "That sounds nice." But that doesn't cut it; something seems missing. It's because it's not a validating response. You would want them to feel like they saw, understood, and shared your excitement. You wanted to evoke the same reaction in her and have a shared experience.

As such, there are a host of easy ways to give *validating responses* versus *invalidating responses*. Remember that when you validate, you are accepting and sharing their emotions.

- That sounds so sad!
- I would be so angry if I was you.
- No wonder you were confused.
- You have every right to be happy.
- I can't blame you for being sad.

Notice how each of these responses refers to an emotion and shows understanding and shared impact. The opposite to these are invalidating responses, which minimize or outright dismiss someone's feelings.

They may stem from the best intentions, but we all know intentions don't count—only actions do.

- It's not a big deal. Don't worry.
- It could be so much worse.
- Look on the bright side.
- Trust me, you'll be fine.
- Yeah, it happens to everyone.

More often than not, these types of responses actually make the situation *worse*. They suggest that the other person is being irrational and/or "shouldn't" feel the way they are—the very *opposite* of how they're hoping to feel by talking with you. Learn to catch these responses and change them into validating ones, and you'll be surprised at the difference it makes.

Validating makes you feel like you're someone's ally in life. There are six steps to validation according to Dr. Marsha Linehan, who created a concept called *dialectal behavior therapy:*

1. Be present. Don't be looking at your phone or doing something else and appearing distracted. Be totally focused on someone as they speak.
2. Summarize what you have heard.
3. Try to put yourself in someone's shoes and guess how he or she feels and thinks. Do this out loud and then ask if you are correct.
4. Think about someone's past and biology. For example, a person who has been abused might be more sensitive to criticism, so understand that when this person reacts poorly to criticism.
5. Tell someone that their emotions are normal and only natural.
6. Try to relate to someone by comparing their experiences to your own to prove that you can feel what they feel.

So for example, when someone is telling you a story about how his coworker upset him, put your phone away and pay attention. Repeat what you have heard to show you are listening. Try to imagine things from his point of view about why that coworker upset him. Consider how he was bullied in school, which could have made him more sensitive to bullying now. Tell him that his reaction is only natural, and relate how you went through the same thing yourself with a rude coworker.

When a person talks, he or she wants to be seen a certain way. He or she also wants a certain reaction. So when you focus on validation, you give them that reaction and subtly say "Yes, I agree with you. You are that person." For example, a guy who is bragging about his car wants to hear "Wow, your car is amazing and I admire how much work you put into it."

A writer named Paul Ford described an interesting concept. When you meet someone, ask what he or she does. Then, when the person tells you, state "Wow, that seems hard." You should do this because most people believe their jobs are difficult. In fact, there is something difficult about everyone's job, so it's not a false belief. By acting as if you think someone's job is hard, you are relating to that person and also showing him or her that you believe just as he or she does. When you say this simple phrase, you agree with a large part of their mental chatter in a way that makes them proud. Plus, it allows people to open up, as complaining is an easy outlet.

Many times throughout this book I have mentioned how important it is to make someone feel good. This is just another form of validation, isn't it? You can accomplish this easily by listening to them and using that time to make someone feel smart and clever.

Take notes as someone speaks. This makes it seem that you really are hanging on every word and value what they are saying. Alternatively, tell people you are going to commit, follow through, or write down what they say at a later point. Obviously, you would only do this with valuable information—and it feels amazing being the source of such information.

Also make remarks that compliment the person. For example, if someone is talking about his most recent academic achievement, say, "Wow, that must have taken tremendous dedication to research! Good job!" Pointing out a person's good qualities and complimenting them based on what they are talking about will stroke his or her ego.

One way to validate someone is to seek his or her advice or input. Ask, "What do you think of this?" before you submit work. Or ask, "You seem to have things in life figured out. Maybe you can help me with my girl problems." You may not want to bother someone, but really, people love giving advice. It makes them feel as if they are important and wise and as if you look up to them as leaders. Bonus if you can ask for advice in something they fancy themselves to be smart in, because that is the ultimate validation of their skills and knowledge.

Later, you can add to this principle by presenting evidence that you followed someone's advice. For example, let them know, "I took your advice about my girlfriend and here's what happened. We worked out our fight and she sent me this sweet text today." There is nothing more validating than seeing a positive outcome from advice you've given.

Finally, when you take note of the smaller things in a conversation, you show how much you are paying attention. Paying attention denotes respect and is therefore an effortless way to flatter someone. You want to remember obscure details or things like dates or personal facts. Later, bring them up again to show that you bothered to pay attention and remember. The person you are talking with will really appreciate that you care so much to listen well and feel that their words had weight.

For example, even remembering something as small as someone's preference for mayonnaise on sandwiches can be impactful. When you get lunch and ask him what he wants, interject as he communicates his order and say, "No mayonnaise, right?"

Listen with Intent

As a general rule of thumb, I try to listen far more than I speak. I do this because I enjoy listening to people's stories, but more importantly, I like to give others *air space* in a conversation. Air space is simply the room to speak without feeling like they are going to be cut off, interrupted, or not share what they wish to share. I find people speak more freely and eagerly when they are given air space.

In some order, here's what people enjoy about conversations: being entertained, speaking and sharing, laughing, and learning something new.

Notice a pattern? If we aren't listening to something we feel has value to us, then we prefer to share about our lives and thoughts. Think about how you feel after you leave a conversation where you don't share much and the air space was monopolized by the other person.

Your neck probably hurt from all that nodding and you felt as if you just left a lecture. You felt neglected. Now imagine a scenario where you were given all the air space you could possibly use and appeared to have a captive audience. You'll come away feeling much different, and that's the type of feeling you should attempt to impart to others by listening with intent.

To become a people person, you need to listen way more than you speak. The sad truth is that it's impossible that everything out of your mouth is going to be fascinating and compelling, so let others share—they'll feel better about themselves and subsequently about you.

There's a giant caveat—to be a good listener, you aren't just giving air space and surrendering your turn to speak. A lot of people think that to be a good listener, you just need to shut up and let the other person talk. While to some extent that's true, there are more parts to the puzzle. That's passive listening. To the other person, it can feel as if they are speaking to a wall.

Active listening is the key to giving others validation. It reads like a mouthful, but it's simple in practice. You are listening with a clear intent.

Let's say that someone says, "Last weekend I was skiing but I wasn't really having a good time." Passive listening would consist of you saying "oh cool" or "uh huh" and only acknowledging their statement and staying silent afterward.

Active listening, and listening with intent, would consist of any of the following:

- *"Didn't have a good time...?"* (Repeating the last phrase of a person's statement)
- *"So you went skiing but it wasn't the best time?"* (Rephrasing their statement back to them)
- *"Sounds like you were expecting a fun and active weekend but something was wrong or missing?"* (Sum up their thoughts and position)

When you read it from the page, it sounds like you might come off like a parrot or a robot. *Active listening is just repeating what someone says? How does that help?*

It helps because people hear far more than simple repetition. They are hearing you use their own words in a new sentence, which gives the strong impression that you were listening intently. It appears that you are following their train of thought with interest. You want to make sure with crystal clarity that you understand them so you can delve deeper.

The best part of all this is the more you do this, the more they will continue to talk and take the conversation into deeper realms. You can literally mix the three types of phrases for an hour and observe in wonder as people pour their hearts out and attempt to explain, justify, and elaborate.

The intent is to crack them open like a nut and learn as much about their inner thought process as possible. People want to feel that they matter. People want to feel that what they have to say is something of consequence—that's the ultimate power of validation. Sound curious and nonjudgmental, as if to ask, "Did I get this right? Please correct me if I did not."

I wasn't sure whether or not I wanted to travel this summer.

Travel this summer?

Yeah, I was thinking about going to Greece but it might be too expensive.

You want to go to Greece minus the prices?

Yeah, I haven't traveled anywhere in the past few years and I've seen so many great pictures of the Greek islands.

Sounds like you need to get away despite the cost!

You could be right. I mean, people are only young once, right? I've always dreamed of traveling the world but work gets in the way.

So work has always gotten in the way?

This conversation could probably continue *ad nauseum*, but notice how all one party is doing is picking and choosing phrases to repeat so that the other party is beckoned to clarify and elaborate further.

It's no wonder that this is the exact technique that psychologists use during therapy sessions to allow people to discover themselves and articulate out loud their inner thoughts. A few well-placed questions in the form of active listening can really crack people open and help them learn about themselves. If you're great at listening with intent, it's impossible for you to become a conversational narcissist.

In most cases, when people share or want to get stuff off their chest, they're looking for a sense of validation. They're not going to get these if you are just going to sit there with a blank expression on your face. Recall that good listening demands active focus and participation.

The most common kinds of emotions people are trying to elicit are excitement, shock, interest, or amusement. These are what you should validate people on. Keep these emotions in mind and make sure to reflect them back—it tells them their message is on point and well received, and it encourages them to share more.

The truth is that listening more enables everything else we are trying to accomplish in this book. When you listen more, you hear feedback from others and how they truly respond to you. When you listen more, you understand people more deeply and what motivates them. When you listen more, you can see if you possess a toxic habit or two.

This skill enables you to get into their world, and all it takes is for you to resist the temptation of interjecting or interrupting.

In the quest to become a better people person, listening well is perhaps the most universal theme—not just according to me. Consider that the following titans of industry made it to the top of their fields not because of their inherent intellect but because of how they were able to work with and lead people. A clear illustration of this point was made by American architect Jeff Daly some years ago: "Two monologues do not make a dialogue."

When you speak with someone, you must make sure that it's a two-way street. It's not a lecture or a sermon. It's an interactive dialogue where two parties collaborate to create something together. Is this what you are creating, or even seeking to create?

Make sure that you are actually listening and engaged, as opposed to ceding the floor and simply waiting for your turn to speak again without acknowledging them. Often, we get the sense that we are only speaking *at* each other instead of *with* each other. If you walk away from a conversation with nothing gained or lost, this is what you've been doing.

Conversations are best viewed as opportunities for learning. They can be opportunities for building bridges instead of each party attempting to show just how intelligent they are. For real dialogue to take place, you have to have an open mind regarding what you can take away from the other person as far as your own personal education is concerned.

Keep an open mind, develop a sense of curiosity, and most importantly, attempt to be less self-centered—this is how you create meaningful and healthy dialogue.

Takeaways:

- The principle of listening well is one that you always hear or read about but probably don't actually engage in. That's because most advice on listening is simply to listen more. That's only part of it.
- To listen better, you should practice your responsiveness. Listening is not a passive activity, and responsiveness is what happens after you process what you have heard. Optimal responsiveness consists of understanding, validating, and caring. The best singular way to

demonstrate responsiveness is to ask questions.

- Listening is a fantastic method of gathering information about yourself. When you observe and monitor others, you gain self-awareness because you can understand how you are being received in multiple facets. Use other people like a mirror to see yourself.
- Validation is another powerful aspect of listening. Validation is when you subtly say, "I see your emotion, share it, and understand it." This is best demonstrated with validating statements, which are emotion-focused, and eliminating invalidating statements, which are incredibly common and serve to dismiss people's emotions.
- Finally, listen with intent to listen better.

Chapter 5: The Principle of Being Valuable

When Sean moved to a new city, he was lonely because he couldn't make any new friends. No one from his work seemed to be interested in becoming friends. He invited them out from time to time but probably not frequently or confidently enough. After three months, his usual weekend plans were still to spend time with his cat and work on his car.

One chance conversation with a coworker uncovered the fact that Sean had a karaoke machine in his home, which he received for

Christmas a few years back. Unbeknownst to Sean, everyone in the office used to be in choir and loved the prospect of recapturing their glory days through karaoke. Friday nights subsequently became known as "karaoke nights at Sean's with Sean and his cat." He quickly became integrated into the office social circle and was able to branch out his groups of friends easily from there.

Where did it all start? It goes beyond the karaoke machine; it's what the karaoke machine represented. It represented some sort of *value* to others that incentivized them to spend time with Sean and get to know him. Without it, who knows how long Sean would have been lonely in his new city.

It's not a lens we like to view relationships through, but it's plainly obvious when you take a step back. Humans are shallow. People operate on a basic transactional basis more than we would like to admit. They like to exchange value and find self-benefit where they can. Put simply, if you can do something for someone, they will like you more. Being able to take part in basic transactions can help you be more likable.

Of course, if a relationship hinges solely upon this value, then it becomes unhealthy. But for initial likability when meeting people, you must determine how you can add value to their lives—it's the most basic currency we care about.

Thankfully, value comes in many forms, so it's not all about having money or the ability to buy gifts. Providing value is about the positive emotions you can give people, and that's a much broader (and kinder) way of viewing value. If you can do something for someone or make them feel a way they want to feel, you are automatically more valuable and hence more likable. If Sean's coworkers only kept him company for his karaoke machine, that is different from the karaoke machine being the initial lure of friendship.

Everyone has needs and desires, and we are usually ignorant or passive to them. The principle of being valuable is about being proactive to people's fundamental human desires—you have them, too, so it's not that difficult to decipher what other people want. Is this manipulative? It might sound like you are trying to bribe people into liking you. That's not quite accurate; you are just understanding how people function instinctually.

The Helpfulness Habit

Adding value to people's lives is essentially being helpful. Get into the habit of thinking how you can proactively help a person to fulfill his needs or desires, both practical, like at work, and emotional, like making them feel good about themselves. People's needs or desires can be primary, or what you can see obviously on the surface, or they can be far more profound and deep— what is below the surface and emotional or psychological in nature.

In the current moment, is there a need or desire someone might have that you can assist with? Probably. It can indeed be a difficult habit to develop, but needs are generally things you can provide that prevent people from feeling a negative emotion, while a desire is something you can provide to cause people to feel a positive emotion.

An example of meeting someone's practical need or desire is helping someone who needs a ride to work. You can provide the ride yourself or you can help them make arrangements for transportation. Because of you, they are able to keep their livelihood. If they have just eaten a greasy hamburger, you might grab them a couple of napkins. If you realize that they haven't eaten lunch, ask if they are hungry or recommend them a restaurant.

An emotional or psychological need or desire is more complex. But just understand that everyone wants to feel loved, respected, and worth something in this world. There are universal themes in what keep us in a good mood versus a bad mood. If you see someone is eating lunch alone at work, this person may be feeling lonely and left out. He or she may feel alienated by coworkers or may be in need for emotional support at the moment. You can make a tremendous difference by asking, "Do you want to join me for lunch?" Reach out to this person and make him or her feel wanted and accepted and fulfill the human desire for company and support.

Now, you can't reasonably spend your whole life serving others, so look for five-minute favors—things you can do in five minutes or less. For example, you can open a door for someone who is struggling with carrying a big box, or you can offer someone a ride on your way to work. Listen to someone for a short amount of time. Shoot someone who is having a rough day a positive text. Think about proactive ways you can help people out that are low effort and investment on your part. You can make a big difference to others without cutting into your own time and needs.

They may be quick to you, but the value of the gesture will be immense and you will cement yourself as the type of person that provides positive value with their presence alone. If you can't do it yourself, provide resources and information that will help people. This will take even less than five minutes but can be of enormous help to someone. Say a person is interested in photography. You don't have to take them under your wing to teach them what you know, but who could you introduce them to that knows photography, and what resources could you curate for them? Anything that can point them in the right direction to fulfilling their needs or desires is adding value.

You don't have to offer help only when people ask for it; most people never ask for help because they are embarrassed and don't want to inconvenience others. This goes beyond offering value; you are anticipating someone's needs and desires. You relieve him or her of the embarrassment of asking, most people's biggest obstacles, and make people's lives easier. Being intuitive makes you more understanding and likable in general. There doesn't have to be a manipulative stigma attached to adding value; you just have to understand that humans are naturally selfish and naturally gravitate toward those who can help us. It's easy to become that person for first impression purposes.

Beyond being helpful, there are a number of ways you can actively add value to people's lives, even passively.

Connect people. Try to be a connector and proactively introduce people for mutually beneficial relationships. If someone needs or desires something, it's not too hard to think of someone who could help out directly or indirectly. As usual, the gesture is worth just as much as the actual connection. Strive to be the person who knows what everyone is good at and can help people make things happen. Your value in this instance is the promise of beneficial connections. There's a reason we hang around with VIPs we don't enjoy personally—because we know we might benefit in some way from being in their presence.

Be the planner. Take on the role of the planner. If you volunteer, it's doubtful anyone will fight you for the privilege since it can often be a hassle. However, your value is actually quite high here. People will begin to look at you and depend on you to make things happen—it quickly becomes a position of leadership and power. Organize get-togethers. Help someone conceive a bachelor party. Plan a vacation for a group, or rent out a room and throw a party. People will like you because you do the hard part and can be relied on for social gatherings and bringing happiness into people's lives.

Have specific knowledge. That way, you can offer people guidance as to what they need to do. This makes you valuable because people look to you for help. This knowledge also gives you inside tips to break the rules in acceptable ways. For example, you might know about national parks, so you can help guide people on where to go and what to wear for a hike. This way, you are valuable because you can help guide people about what to do. In a similar vein, have expertise on obscure issues.

Know about things that others don't so that you can be a source of information that no one else has. You might be the only person who knows how to program a computer, and then everyone will be calling on you to help them with computer troubles. If you know something obscure, you will be the only authority on the subject and people will want to know you as a result to get help on the matter.

Be entertaining. Recall that value isn't limited to things with monetary value; value is about addressing people's needs or desires to create positive feelings. Therefore, value can be entertainment as well. In fact, it's one of the forms of value that most influence everyday friendships and relationships. You may not see eye to eye politically with your best friend, and they may borrow money from you constantly and never pay you back, but if they make you laugh and are fun to be around, their relative value is great enough to continue spending time with them.

Indeed, most friendships are formed simply because people enjoy being around each other. That is value in its purest form—if I spend time with someone and know I will be happy and laugh, I will gravitate toward them. This can take the form of compelling conversation, captivating anecdotes, humorous observations, or jokes. You don't have to be the life of the party; being entertained is a purely subjective matter.

Everyone likes different types of movies, and movies are almost always preferred to dry lectures—because they are entertaining. Thus, entertainment as value makes you magnetic.

Entertain people by focusing on them, their interests, and their lives. Entertain people by understanding and being familiar with current events so you can have an engaging and thoughtful dialogue. Further entertain them by being understanding of different histories and cultures so you can add context into any conversation. Entertain people by giving knowledge they seek or soliciting knowledge from them and thrusting them into the pleasing role of a teacher. Entertain by being more spontaneous, asking people hypothetical questions, and being less predictable.

Providing value to people by being entertaining is actually advice about how to be a better conversationalist in disguise, isn't it? It diverges from typical conversation advice because it takes you out of the equation and asks you to focus on others and how you can prioritize their needs. When you realize that successful relationships don't begin with focusing on you, and instead should be weighted toward others, it necessarily requires that you have a different approach.

The principle of providing value may sound a bit insensitive and transactional at the outset, but remember, it's not that we are bribing people to like us. If our goal is to become likable, we would be smart to recognize that being a useful, helpful, and valuable person is going to increase your perceived charm more often than not. At the very least, you will make yourself attractive enough to gain entry—and sometimes we just need the opportunity to shine, like Sean and his karaoke machine from earlier in this chapter.

Takeaways:

- The principle of being valuable can sound insensitive and transactional, but it simply plays on the fact that humans are selfish creatures. We are, initially at least, motivated to spend time with those who we perceive as valuable. Value isn't just money-related, thank goodness.
- Being valuable is about how to be helpful and add to people's lives and impart positive feelings. You can do this by addressing people's practical needs and desires or their emotional needs and desires. The realistic way of doing this is to think about five-minute favors for people.

- Additional ways of adding value are being a social connector, being the planner of a group, and focusing on providing entertainment (in the same way that people enjoy going to a movie).
- This principle underscores an important theme of considering others and not approaching people from a self-centered perspective.

Chapter 6: The Principle of Shallowness

Rick showed up for a job interview in a sloppy, stained outfit with his hair messy. He seemed rushed and unprepared. He also didn't smell great, as if he had skipped showering before rushing to the interview. As a result, he made a poor first impression before he even opened his mouth and didn't get the job. He was actually the most qualified candidate by far, but that didn't matter.

After Rick, Derek walked in for the next interview. He was well groomed, shaved, and had neatly styled hair. He wore a nice suit. He was presentable and though his skills weren't as impressive as Rick's, he was offered the job immediately.

Further, Derek never understood why he was able to get jobs when better-qualified people like Rick couldn't. Practically any interview Derek walked into, he walked out with a job offer. Does this mean that life is not a meritocracy?

Unfortunately, it's not. Humans operate heavily on a first impression, which is governed by things that are bound to make you feel shallow. We are judged to be likable or not in a split second. The principle of shallowness recognizes this and sheds light on how we can use it to our advantage like Derek might.

This principle is about understanding what humans look for instinctually. We value appearance and other superficial factors highly. It's not all bad, though. If you know what humans tend to focus on, even if you disagree in principle, then you know exactly what to do for likability and a great first impression. You will know how to tweak your appearance and follow certain rules to have appeal.

Don't underestimate how powerful the first impression is. Once yours is created, it's unlikely you will be able to change it without considerable time and effort. That's because a first impression creates a lens for people to view you through. Whatever they see that complies with their impression confirms it further, and whatever they see that doesn't comply with their impression is just an anomaly that isn't representative of your true character. It will color how someone views and treats you.

A bad first impression can kill a relationship of any kind before it can even start, while a good first impression gives you a green light to proceed and get to know someone better. We've been taught not to focus on shallow and superficial traits since we were young, but it turns out we shouldn't necessarily follow that advice.

First Impression Management

Fortunately, you can tweak your appearance to make the best first impression possible. Just a few changes will result in a huge shift in how people receive you.

A study conducted at Princeton University discovered that people make snap judgments about someone's personality, likability, and trustworthiness within a fraction of a second of seeing someone's face. Janine Willis and Alexander Todorov found that people tend to judge trustworthiness within 100 milliseconds of meeting someone. Furthermore, these judgments tended to stick and were extremely difficult to alter. Ask yourself if this is going to benefit or harm you. This is why it's important to give in to something seemingly so trivial and silly. If we take our goal to make better impressions versus stick with our principles that a book should not be judged by its cover, then we can instantly see what we should do.

For instance, a first impression can be formed just by someone seeing you for the first time while you are scowling. Will they assume that you are a negative person or unpleasant to be around? It sounds outrageous, but it's entirely possible. That negative judgment will always haunt you; thus, your impression will forever be based on a scowl you wore one day while you were briefly in a bad mood.

Before we delve into the meat of this content, researcher Frank Schab identified six common ways we judge and stereotype people based on their physical appearances. These six ways emphasize just how many conclusions we jump to are based on a single trait.

1. Looking physically attractive: "This person is healthy and more attractive than me."
2. Speaking faster: "This person is more competent and intelligent than most others."
3. An easy gait: "This person is confident and trustworthy."

4. A baby face: "This person is trustworthy."
5. Dressing smartly: "This person is successful and smart."
6. Multiple tattoos: "This person is promiscuous, unreliable, and untrustworthy."

Five out of those six factors are controllable—the only one that is not is whether or not you have a relatively rounded baby face. You might be thinking that being physically attractive is out of your control, but that can also be a product of wardrobe, grooming, and effort. Besides tweaking the above factors, making a good first impression is largely grounded upon *who* you want to impress.

According to a study conducted by Turk, Swencionis, and Fiske, there are *downward* comparisons where you outrank someone else and *upward* comparisons where the person outranks you. When making downward comparisons, you should try to appear more nice and agreeable. On the other hand, in upward comparisons, you try to appear more competent.

If you're higher in status, it is more effective to attempt to prove that you're not as cold as the stereotype would suggest, while if you are lower in status, it is better to show that they are as smart or smarter than those above them in status. Making the best impression is more than just looking good; it's about making the other person perceive you as well as possible according to your status. You need to adapt accordingly. Appearing too smart can make the other person feel outranked, belittled, or intimidated, while appearing too nice can make you seem weak and passive, so you want to emphasize what is best for your position.

You may not be overly surprised at what we've uncovered about first impressions thus far. We already know the general importance of maintaining eye contact, open posture, and confident body language in first impressions. We know we shouldn't fidget or shift side to side because it makes us look untrustworthy. We generally know how someone looks when they appear trustworthy and when they appear like someone we wouldn't want to encounter in a dark alley. We have covered the basics of what will make you excel in a job interview. But what else can we learn about that is less obvious, just as important, and likely new?

Voice Pitch

The pitch of your voice can add to the first impression you make. Pitch, of course, refers to how high or low your voice is.

Research out of the University of Glasgow from McAleer, Todorov, and Belin in 2014 found that people made snap judgments in milliseconds about someone just by hearing their voices. Men and women who spoke in higher pitches were often deemed more trustworthy by study participants. Meanwhile, researchers out of the University of Miami (Klofstad, Anderson & Peters, 2012) found that both men and women tend to associate lower-pitched voices with leadership and select leaders accordingly.

The researchers noted, "Because women, on average, have higher-pitched voices than men, voice pitch could be a factor that contributes to fewer women holding leadership roles than men." McAleer and his colleagues advise that "People and algorithms may be instructed on the necessary alterations to obtain a desired projection."

In other words, learning to control your pitch may be a powerful tool for making the right first impression. Since pitch relates to making a good first impression, you want to control and influence your pitch accordingly. So if you want to get a job in upper management, speak with a more masculine and deep voice at the interview.

Lower pitch might be better because it is traditionally associated with masculine and leadership qualities. Then again, you might not be in a position where you want to appear assertive and dominant. Again, it's best to tailor your characteristics for the impression that you want.

Handshake

People form judgments about you based on your handshake worldwide. There are some important Western guidelines to how you should shake hands to present yourself in the best way possible.

If you still don't believe that a mere handshake should matter that much, a 2008 study on handshakes found that people with stronger handshakes were often chosen for the job over those with weaker handshakes. Evidently, you can make a good impression with a nice, firm grip. Don't underestimate handshakes!

There are three factors that play into a good handshake that will earn you brownie points with others:

1. **Firm**. A good handshake should be firm but not hand-crushing; just squeeze firmly.
2. **Warm**. A warm hand signals a warm personality and a cold one signals a cold personality. That's ridiculous, but it's

how our brains operate—by association. So keep your hands warm and you're in.

3. **Dry**. A dry hand means you're not sweaty or clammy. Not being sweaty means you're calm and confident.

Before you shake someone's hand, rub it in your pocket to warm it up and dry it off. Then give a firm handshake, applying some pressure.

Wardrobe

How you dress speaks volumes to others. You don't want to dress the wrong way or dress sloppily. But overdressing can be bad, too. Despite the age-old advice to dress to impress, you don't always want to do this, especially if you are dressing more nicely than the other person. Being overdressed can imply that you possess authority, which can really make it awkward if you are meeting with somebody who is supposed to be *your* authority. It can create an off-putting power struggle that will ultimately make people think, "Who do they think they are?"

You can think of adjusting your wardrobe similarly to how you should address whether to emphasize competence or niceness. What you wear definitely says something about you and your intentions, so you should be mindful of the company you will keep.

You can always follow this rule of thumb: dress *similarly* to who you want to make an impression on. Dressing similarly is not only appealing; it makes people assume that you understand them and think similarly to them. It also avoids the potential negative implications if you dress much better or much worse. When it comes to making a warm and welcoming first impression, people want to see you're *like* them, not better or worse than them.

Takeaways:

- This is a principle about our sad reality. We are shallow creatures, though we might not like to admit it or play the game. Thus, how can we shore up our physical appearance and make a better shallow impression?

- Studies have identified at least six judgments people make based purely on physical appearance such as having a "baby face," an easy gait, dressing well, and speaking quickly. Studies also showed that it depends on who you are talking to in terms of relative status. If you are talking to someone of lower status, a better impression will depend on appearing nice. If you are talking to someone of higher status, a better impression will depend on appearing competent.

- Vocal pitch has also been shown to make a difference, impression-wise. A higher-pitched voice has been associated with trustworthiness, while a lower-pitched voice has been associated with authority and leadership.

- This should come as no surprise; a handshake's characteristics are used to stereotype and judge—at least in Western cultures. Finally, wardrobe can make a difference as to how you are perceived. Dressing too well or too poorly can open a can of worms; thus, it is a good policy to dress similarly to who you want to make an impression on so you can get the benefit of the doubt.

Chapter 7: The Principle of Empathy

Marshall was always a rather frigid person. He thought about his own emotions but never tried to understand how or why others might feel the way that they do. As a result, he often would offend or insult people, even in everyday conversation. He didn't mean to, but he lacked the capability to put himself in other people's shoes and try to imagine what others might feel from his words. He got into a lot of fights, and though most of them were small and meaningless, it didn't win him many friends. The friends he did have tended to ignore this side of Marshall and nicknamed him "the robot."

Marshall's brother, Andrew, was the opposite. Somehow he had attained the ability to imagine the emotions other people might be feeling. Andrew was popular and people felt that they could talk to him. He never offended people or dismissed their emotions as his brother did. Often he would clean up his brother's messes and talk to Marshall and point out why people got so mad at him. He attempted to teach Marshall how to change his ways. One particular instance involved Andrew explaining to Marshall why he shouldn't have told a female friend to simply lose weight when she asked how she was going to fit into a dress for a certain occasion.

Had Marshall followed Andrew's example and made the effort to embody empathy, he might have had more friends. Learning and using empathy is not just a way to avoid fights and deepen friendships. It is the capacity to understand exactly what people are feeling and why and to calibrate yourself to generate more positivity and likability.

It grants you the ability to understand and share the feelings of another person. You can relate to how the person feels, even if you have never experienced the same thing yourself. If you can't relate, then at least you can understand logically what they are feeling and why. For instance, if someone seems down after seeing a girl kissing another boy, you can bet that he likes that girl and feels sad that she has chosen another boy to be with. If someone is crying but has just won an award, you can imagine that he or she is crying tears of pride and joy, not of sadness. The skill of empathy allows you to assess situations and make well-informed guesses as to the emotional landscape and causations.

It shows others how you truly understand people and at least can appear to know what they are thinking or how they feel. We like people who understand us and speak the same language. This similarity helps us relate to each other. We already talked about how emotions are important in likability. In this principle, we will hone in on how you can use empathy and emotional intelligence to relate to people on a deeper level.

For our purposes, empathy and *emotional intelligence* are relatively interchangeable. They both concern awareness of emotions and causations. Emotional intelligence is having the ability to effectively perceive, control, and evaluate emotions in yourself as well as in others. To be emotionally intelligent means having the ability to empathize with others, which subsequently helps you to better understand people's deepest needs. You display emotional intelligence when you become aware of the emotions you are experiencing. However, awareness is only a start. You must also show that you understand these emotions and the impact that they have on your state-of-mind. Moreover, you need to recognize how your emotions are affecting the people around you. You also display emotional intelligence when recognizing another person's emotions. In other words, when you empathize with another person, you are displaying emotional intelligence.

It can be said to consist of four distinct but interrelated parts.

- Self-awareness: awareness of yourself and of your emotional experiences, while understanding how your emotions impact your behavior.
- Self-management: having an ability to control your emotional impulses through the simultaneous processing of other emotions.
- Social awareness: understanding how to empathize and relate to people; understanding people's needs and concerns.
- Social management: the ability to communicate your emotions and needs while recognizing and respecting those of other people.

Empathy is additionally important because it enables you to apply *emotional management*. Emotional management is where you determine how someone is feeling and react appropriately. For example, if someone is happy but crying after winning an award, you don't want to rush to help the person cheer up because the person isn't sad. You want to adjust your behavior according to someone's emotions, and you can only do that by learning to empathize. Very rarely will people tell you how they are truly feeling, especially negative states, so you must put yourself in their shoes and judge how they would probably feel based on the situation.

This creates situations where people will express themselves and you will just understand. To be empathetic, here are specific guidelines to focus on.

Focus on what is good for others. Don't just think about yourself. Ask, "Will this hurt so and so? What are the possible negative repercussions for people other than me?" For example, you want to go out and party but your wife is feeling sick. Will going out hurt her feelings? Is this going to be worth whatever enjoyment you derive from going out? You might consider staying home to take care of her. Think about how you may hurt others and what you can do to be better—this is a surprisingly simple step that most of us neglect sometimes. Try to do more good than harm and understand that your actions have consequences.

Think about shared experiences. Many feelings and sentiments are universal. If someone loses a dear friend, for example, you know how that person probably feels since you have been through loss yourself. Thus, we are not all so different after all and you can use your own experiences to help you understand others. Try to guess how someone is feeling based on what you have felt and been through before. You may not have lost a dear friend, but you can perhaps imagine when you lost a pet or suffered a huge defeat—they aren't the same magnitude, but you are closer than you were before to understanding someone's mental state of being. Guessing how others are feeling based on your own values helps you understand how to treat someone.

Don't judge others. You don't know their full story. When you see a homeless person on the street, don't just assume he put himself there or is a hopeless drug addict who doesn't deserve your loose change. We often make judgments based on incomplete or flat-out wrong information driven by assumptions. Get the full story before you make a decision about someone. Just imagine how you might feel if someone judged you based on your worst moment. Once you know the full story, you may be inclined to be more understanding and kind.

Use someone else's perspective. Maybe you don't understand why someone would react as he did when you made a joke. You didn't mean any offense but he took it that way. Try to look at it from his perspective, compendium of experiences, current state of mind, and background. What about the joke may have hit a sensitive spot? Just because someone takes a different approach than you does not mean that he is wrong. He just sees things differently based on a very reasonable set of justifications.

Try to see how others approach the world and why they do what they do instead of just assuming they are wrong because they differ from your current perspective.

Ask open-ended questions. Get someone to talk to you by asking questions that demand more than yes or no answers, such as "How do you feel today?" or "Why did you feel the need to do that? Do you feel that was the appropriate way to react?" This is when you're in information-gathering mode. By asking these questions, you can directly hear about someone's emotions and causes for said emotions. There's nothing better than hearing it straight from the horse's mouth; you might even gain something from the way they say things and what they didn't say. Simple yes or no questions allow a person to avoid disclosing emotional information. Open-ended questions let people respond with a story and narrative about how things came to be. This is much more important than knowing that someone is happy or sad or angry.

Self-disclose. If someone doesn't want to talk, you might share a bit about yourself to make him feel more comfortable. For example, say, "How do you feel?" When he refuses to answer, go on: "Well, to be honest with you, I feel pretty horrible about all this." He will feel more open to sharing when you already have made yourself vulnerable. Do this to get the ball rolling and create a space of safety for sharing. You might just discover that you have quite a few feelings in common.

Find neutral ground. Don't be overly friendly or overly cold. Don't be one extreme or the other. The more neutral you are, the less extreme you seem. This can make the other person trust you more and feel more at ease sharing things with you. For example, when talking to someone after a fight and trying to empathize to strike a resolution, don't smile or frown, don't appear threatening or overly affectionate, relax your body to avoid conveying aggression, use a soft middle tone that is neither yelling nor whispering, and keep appropriate space. Doing this helps you appear less like an enemy or a friend, but rather just somebody he can talk to without fear of judgment. Surprisingly, being completely on someone's side as a close confidant is not always the best move because you'll be acting in a way to confirm their beliefs instead of airing and hearing them out. This can create an overly emotionally charged situation and prolong negativity instead of alleviating it.

Don't run ahead of the conversation. This is where you jump to the ending point or conclusion of a discussion on emotions without partaking in the intermediate steps—those are the important steps. You acknowledge the *situation* but don't recognize the feelings involved. Even if you see no point in discussing feelings, people often have to talk and work things out for themselves to understand what you see from an objective bystander perspective. For instance, this is when someone tells you they recently ended a relationship and you reply with "That sucks, but there are plenty of fish in the sea!" This well-meaning advice is actually detrimental (and invalidating) because it ignores the emotions and jumps immediately to the conclusion that they must seek out new fish. This is obvious, but it's not what they need to hear at the moment to feel empathized with.

So instead of jumping to conclusions and skipping the seemingly extraneous part of asking how they feel, connect with people on their current emotional state and then gently move them to the point you are already mentally at. You could rectify the same situation with the friend who ended a relationship by asking how it happened and how they feel about it. Eventually, you can slowly guide them toward their plans for coping and discovering new species of fish.

Practice. The more you practice, the better you will get. Try to use empathy in every situation. Even when your mother is mad and yelling about the dishes, try to imagine how she must feel to come into a room with a sink full of dishes after she has been working all day long. It is a habit to build up, and research has shown that habits can take at least two months to create. The point of practicing is to make empathy an unconscious habit you automatically apply to the people around you.

Empathy doesn't consist of a small workload, but it is worth the closeness you can build with someone when they feel that you care about them and understand them intuitively. In reality, you may have just been taking informed guesses based on your own experiences, but that doesn't ultimately matter. The principle of empathy is one of your most powerful yet subtle weapons in likability.

Takeaways:

- The principle of empathy is the principle of understanding people's emotional states, the causes, and how you have the potential to contribute negatively or positively. For our purposes, emotional intelligence is mostly interchangeable. Emotional intelligence is similarly about the understanding of causes of emotions in all parties present and consists of self-awareness, self-management, social awareness, and social management.

- Empathy is important because it allows you to generate positive and likable outcomes with people on account of understanding their mental states of being. There are a few ways to grow your powers of empathy. These include focusing on what is good for others, thinking about shared values and experiences, not judging others, stepping into other people's perspective and unique set of circumstances, asking open-ended questions to gather information, self-disclosing, using neutral ground and creating an optimal space for sharing, not jumping to the end of the conversation, and practicing it until it becomes an unconscious habit.

Chapter 8: The Principle of Abrasiveness

Sally was shy so she didn't talk to people after meeting them the first time. She was also quite anxious and nervous, so she didn't tend to reply if people followed up, reached out, or invited her to social events. When she did talk to people, she didn't listen much and she liked to steal the spotlight since she had so few opportunities to feel listened to. You can guess how this impacted Sally's social opportunities. They dwindled quickly because people grew annoyed at her and felt that she was a rather abrasive presence rather than an enjoyable one.

Things changed when she stopped relying on others to build her social network for her. This means she began to change her listening behaviors and initiate contact with people more and more. She even invited people over to her home for a dinner party and was pleasantly surprised when everyone she invited accepted. More importantly, she let people talk and focused on hearing them out rather than planning how she would steal the attention. She noticed a huge change in how people related to her.

It seems obvious enough, right? You must avoid being *unlikable* if you want to be likable.

Most of us have toxic, annoying, and repellent habits. Most of them are harmless enough, but every once in a while, you'll come across someone you simply can't stand on the basis of one of their behaviors. Hopefully it's unintentional on their part, but the point is that being abrasive and annoying can overshadow all of your good traits. Hence, the principle of abrasiveness is about momentarily ignoring the fact that we should try to be likable—we should also focus our efforts on eliminating our unlikable, abrasive behaviors. They can matter more than any amount of charm or charisma you might have.

There are probably various bad, unlikable, or repulsive habits that you hold in your personality without even realizing it. Those who get to know you find that you are awesome, but how many people will bother to break through your exterior facade and get to know the real you? Not many, because as we know, people base their likability on their first impressions of you, and if they don't care for the first impression you give, they won't bother investing more time in you.

This principle might sound like being a filtered version of yourself is the best way to be likable, but that's not the point. The more accurate interpretation is that you should be yourself, but if *yourself* tends to alienate people, then that's probably something to improve. You aren't changing; rather, you're improving.

For instance, Sally was shy and anxious, but these aren't necessarily negative traits. Her abrasive trait was her tendency to steal people's thunder. If someone does this once or twice, others may not even notice it or care. But if this becomes a pattern of behavior, there is a cumulative effect and people will simply start avoiding you, no matter if your stories are the best or you have the most hilarious jokes. People will begin to associate you more heavily with negativity and annoyance, despite your admirable traits.

Unintentional abrasiveness can be easily averted.

One-Sided Relationships

A one-sided relationship is where you are a passive participant. You make the other person, presumably your friend, do everything, take on the burden, and plan everything. Not only that, you depend on your friend for the entire upkeep of the relationship. This likely isn't because you don't feel like people are worth your time; it's likely because you don't realize what a normal, healthy relationship should look like. Namely, it should look relatively equal in terms of effort and time invested.

This also goes back to the principle of being valuable. If you aren't reaching out or making an effort, what value are you presenting to people? You are actually making people's lives more frustrating and inconvenienced for the privilege of spending time with you. That's an easy way to stop getting invited to social activities. Make plans and shoulder the burden of building and upkeeping a relationship.

This is an easy step to logically understand, but it's harder follow through on. Make your calendar work for you and set up reminders for how often you should reach out to people, plan something, or even just say hello. You might even take the extra step of marking in your calendar who reached out last, just so you can visually see that you aren't dropping the ball. It can be as easy as a quick text to ask how someone is doing. Otherwise, you run the risk of sitting back while someone does the hard work and only reaching out when you have something you want from others. This becomes painfully transparent quickly, and people will understand that you aren't willing to put in effort toward them.

Don't flake. Your friend makes plans with you to go out at 6:00. You put time, money, and effort into getting ready. Just when the clock hits 5:57, your friend calls and says, "Sorry, but I'm not feeling well. I don't think I'll go tonight. But have fun!" It feels awkward and disappointing when someone flakes. You don't have to power through social events and torture yourself, but try to let people know as far ahead of time as possible.

Flaking is easy, especially as a busy adult. You get excited for something, then when the time comes, work and kids and other responsibilities have you so tired that you can't muster the energy or the will to go.

Canceling plans is so tempting, but not only is it abrasive no matter how you do it, it also erodes people's trust in you. When you show your reliability, you build trust. Flaking is all about you and wholly inconsiderate to other people.

Provide mutual support. A common way that relationships are one-sided is in how much support is given and received. If you're a good friend, you celebrate people's successes and help them deal with their failures. You can probably sense when they need support and help. However, does this person only interact with you when they need support and not seek you out when you need it? This can even be when you have great news and they don't congratulate you.

Instead of jumping in and hijacking conversations with your problems and complaints, recognize when people have something to say. This is easy because all you have to do is give them the conversational space and silence to speak their mind and then ask questions of them—and resist talking about yourself. So when someone tells you that he is looking into a new house, don't start spouting your opinions on the housing market and lamenting how your salary will never allow you to buy a house.

There is obviously a reason they made that statement, and you shouldn't discount that they either have something they want to get off their chest or want to ask you for advice. Acknowledge what he says and let him finish speaking before you put your two cents in. Stay on target and make it clear that the focus is on them. Don't be a conversational narcissist and use conversation as your vehicle to shine—if you approach them with that intention, you will surely be unlikable. Again, we run into the theme of being proactive with people's needs and looking outside of yourself.

Provide *mutual* emotional support. A common problem is when one friend is used as an emotional crutch for the other, but when the time comes for reciprocation, suddenly the first friend is nowhere to be found. This is the very epitome of a one-sided relationship. A friendship is meant to benefit and enrich two people, so don't be the selfish, emotionally draining friend that only takes and doesn't give back to the common good. Don't be a fair-weather friend and only be there for the good times or when you need some support.

Congratulate someone on good news. Cheer them up when they are sad. Talk them through their pain when they are mad or sad. Dig deep, even, to find out what is troubling someone and try to fulfill one of your main friendship duties of *being there for them*. Finally, never dismiss or ignore their emotions. And certainly never tell them not to feel the way that they feel. They have a right to feel a certain way, and your job as a friend is to listen, not to argue or dismiss.

In a similar vein, don't use people. When you use someone, you befriend them for some benefit you foresee, and you may not actually care about them or like them; you may tolerate them, but that's surely not the basis for a strong friendship. Sooner or later, you will get caught. People may fall for being used a time or two, but they will get wise to it if you are using them only for your own gain. It really hurts to be used like a tool.

One thing many people fail to realize is that their reputations precede them. Avoid only contacting people when you need something. Maybe you do care for a friend or family member, but you only call them up when you need something. It gets to the point where they answer your calls with "What do you need?" If you find yourself only calling someone when you need a favor or you are bored and need attention, try to break the cycle and just call to chat. You never need a reason to call or text someone. You can just check in now and then.

When someone does something for you, be kind and pay it forward. In fact, make it a point to equalize matters. Pay back your debts when they lend you money, return favors, and always offer to help them as they have helped you. If a friend treats you to dinner, take note and treat them the next time you two go out together. Otherwise, you are a moocher, a leech, and you drain people dry by taking from them without giving back. Friends do things for each other, but one-sided friendships where only person does things for the other are unbalanced and unhealthy. Soon, the person who does everything will start to resent you for all the debt you have built up. Avoiding this debt in the first place is a sign that you respect others and don't see them as piggy banks to borrow or steal from.

Recognize People's Limitations

Imagine that someone asked you to do something you weren't comfortable with. Maybe a friend back in high school asked you to shoplift. *Or imagine if someone wants to hang out constantly but you need your space and time away from people.* You may feel obligated to do what this person wants just to please him or her because you are friends and friends do things for each other. But when asked to do what you don't want to do, you feel very pressured and even suffocated. You get antsy and uncomfortable. What do you do? Your friend put you in a tough situation where you probably ended up resenting them. But do we do the same to others?

You must learn people's limitations and boundaries. Crossing them will make someone feel like you do when people asked you to shoplift. Overstaying your welcome and acting too dependent and clingy is a real problem in relationships, old and new. People need space, and their definition of space is probably not the same as yours.

A person's limitations are parameters on the amount of interaction they feel comfortable with. Someone may not be able to hang out on Fridays because of work commitments, for example, or they may not be able to play squash with you because of a torn rotator cuff injury. Being mindful of what someone can and cannot do helps you figure out how to spend time with the person in a way that is feasible for both of you.

It requires some sacrifice and compromise sometimes, but if you care for the person, you will do that, no questions asked. If you were to imagine that person's boundaries were set in stone and that grave injury would come to them if you violated them, you might act differently—the problem, is we see people's boundaries as malleable and persuadable. If you ignore or violate someone's limitations, you make him or her uncomfortable and strain the friendship. Being overly disrespectful of someone's limitations can hurt him or her to the point of not liking you at all anymore. This is important for you to self-police because not everyone is capable of being assertive and saying no to their friends.

A person's boundaries are steadfast rules that dictate what the person is willing to do or willing to tolerate. One friend might not mind you touching him and hugging him, while another friend hates touch and doesn't allow much more than a handshake.

Many people have boundaries about lending you money or doing you favors. Boundaries are in place to protect someone's interests and well-being from others. When you violate someone's boundaries, you hurt that person. Respect boundaries as hard rules that you are absolutely never allowed to violate. For whatever reason, we tend to treat those closest to us as if they have malleable boundaries—a strange reward for closeness.

Don't Force It

Don't force too many friendships. Trying to be super popular means that you are spreading yourself too thin. You don't have enough of yourself to give to everyone, which means everyone will suffer from a fraction of your undivided attention. Or as you try to please and entertain and talk to everyone, one person may eat up the majority of your attention, leaving only table scraps for everyone else. This is going to be detrimental, especially if you set the wrong expectations with people and then continually fail to live up to them. You can't be everything to everyone, so it's a disservice to your friends to try. And of course, it is supremely unlikable because you make people feel like second-class citizens, or last resorts, or fallback plans all the time.

For example, at any social gathering, you will notice that you can have deep conversations with only so many people in one given night. Or you can have a number of shallow and brief conversations with literally everyone at the party. You will ignore a lot of the guests if you just focus on those few deep conversations, but these types of interactions, not the shallow interactions, actually create friendship. It's the same principle when you are trying to be with too many friends at once. You can really only have a few deep friendships; three to five is a realistic number. You can give your A+ effort to that many people. If you try to please more, then you will fail, and all of your friends will suffer. Don't force it. The three to five number may remain the same, but the people that inhabit it are likely to be constantly changing throughout your life.

Another thing to not force is friendships in general. This might be an odd statement, but the fact is, we are not destined to be close with everyone we come across. Some people are only meant to be acquaintances and some people are meant to be passing friends or friends of convenience. Generally, there are three types of friends that people in your life will fall into: inner circle or close friends who know the details of your personal life and talk to regularly; regular friends whom you like and whom you meet up with now and then and who know a bit about you but not the very personal details; and acquaintances who are not close to you and know little about you but will help you out or engage in friendly banter when they see you.

So you might have your two best friends, whom you have known since you shared a dorm in college. Then you have your regular friends, Fred and Susan, whom you meet up with on weekends to go bowling. Finally, you have countless acquaintances, at work, at church, at the bowling alley, and at the gym, where you chat and banter for a few minutes. You remember their names but can't really remember the names of all of their kids or their spouses.

There are so many reasons why friends may not ever advance beyond their normal point. It is usually not personal. People may intersect paths for a brief moment in time but drastically change trajectories afterward. You may want to be friends with someone based on what they represent but not who they are. You may simply find that you only work well together in certain contexts, and interactions don't go so smoothly outside of those contexts. Whatever the case, you may not feel the pull to upgrade this person to the next level of friendship, no matter how cool they are objectively or to other people. And that's okay. Don't force it.

A big factor in friendship incompatibility is varying levels of social appetites. Maybe someone has a social appetite to stay in while you prefer to go out, so you two have difficulties finding time when you both can hang out doing something you both enjoy. You might be the person that wants to hang out with somebody once a week, but they might be the person that wants social time once a month (or every day). Since it is statistically unlikely that you exactly match, you will almost always be either "overdoing it" or "underdoing it." There is no perfect solution to this except to be nice but honest about this.

You cannot force a friendship if you don't match someone the right way, and forcing it will only cause you to fake it and change yourself unnecessarily. Just accept the friendship as it is meant to be naturally, whatever stage it ends up in.

THINK

Finally, in the principle of abrasiveness, it's important to simply not be abrasive. The previous points in this chapter were about the ways in which you might indirectly turn people off. But abrasiveness is also just the way you speak to others and the words you use. As such, it may be productive to run your thoughts through a filter conveniently called the *THINK* acronym. Before you speak, use THINK and evaluate what you're about to say.

Is it True? Make only comments that are true—true to what you feel, true to your beliefs, and true to what you know about the world. When everyone communicates in truth, it allows us to forge connections in openness and trust. If it's not true, what is your purpose in saying it? It will likely just result in miscommunication and eventual tension. Speaking untruths and lies will get you caught eventually and makes you appear manipulative.

Is it Helpful? Give helpful comments, especially when someone is asking for your opinion or advice. Speak with the intention to help and assist people with their needs or desires. This stands in stark contrast to the intention to question, confuse, or tear people down. Think about the purpose of your statements and ask whether you are making them to help people or to feel better about yourself in some way. As we know, if you seek to help, you become someone with value.

Is it Inspiring? Is what you say going to trigger people into action? And if it is, is it going to be through a positive way, or is it going to be fear-based or manipulative? Inspiring is when you cheer people on, inject positivity into their lives, and make them feel capable. Again, this goes to your intentions when speaking to others—are you trying to make them feel good about themselves or bad? If you find that you're not inspiring, you are probably making them feel bad. Providing emotional support is inspiring.

Is it Necessary? Is it necessary that someone hear what you are saying? This can work in two ways. First, if you are delivering negative feedback, just how much is necessary to get your point across? Deliver that and stop immediately, because nothing else is necessary and just serves to hurt people. If it's not necessary, then pick your battles and shut your mouth. Second, are you talking about topics that matter or are you staying on shallow formalities? The latter is unnecessary and empty.

Is it Kind? This speaks to the old adage that "If you can't say anything nice, don't say anything at all." People judge, criticize, and insult without a second thought. This is increasingly popular as we become more and more accustomed to Internet anonymity. With every comment you make, strive to examine what your purpose is and what the impact will be. Chances are, if you're not speaking to be kind, you're speaking out of maliciousness or uncontained emotion. Strive to be kind and use kind words and compliments in abundance.

This might seem like a heavy filter to use, but it's not meant to be used simultaneously, all the time. The value of THINK is to gain self-awareness through the act of asking ourselves questions and examining our intentions. Hopefully it becomes habitual over time to consider the abrasiveness and impact of your words on others. And of course, if you run through these questions and find that more often than not you aren't THINKing, it's time to either change your thought patterns or be more accepting of silence. We constantly speak simply to fill space and avoid awkwardness, but that can be more detrimental than beneficial.

Filtering yourself in this way doesn't have to feel forced or artificial. All you're doing is making sure you have the emotional impact you want on others; if you want to have a negative one, then by all means carry on!

Takeaways:

- Although it may not seem like it, this is an extremely important chapter. Sometimes it pays to be less abrasive and annoying than charming. Charming may open doors for you, but being abrasive and unlikable will shut them even more quickly.
- Most of the ways we are abrasive and unlikable are relatively indirect. They

are actions that make people want to avoid us and stop contact. One such way is maintaining one-sided relationships in terms of effort, emotional support, and time invested. If this occurs, then you may become known as someone who reaches out only when they want something: a user. Be sure to proactively provide emotional support to others, especially if you have just unloaded your emotions onto someone else.

- Recognize that everyone has different limitations and don't overstay your welcome. This applies to all avenues but especially social appetites and desire for interaction. Everyone has their own boundaries, so don't try to force past them because you'll only be met with annoyance and resentment.

- Finally, use the THINK acronym to evaluate your words and their impact on people to not be abrasive. THINK stands for True, Helpful, Inspiring, Necessary, and Kind. Get into the habit of running your thoughts through this type of filter for increased likability.

Chapter 9: The Principle of Worthiness

Jeffrey usually has a lot to say. He reads the news every morning and always seems to be consuming media whenever he has free time. He avoids gossip sites and reality television, but he generally learns a few facts each day. No wonder he can connect and relate with people on just about any topic that comes up.

Furthermore, he is able to offer his perspectives on the topic. Other people might just answer with one-word replies and not offer insight or analysis. Jeffrey is a blast to talk to because he always seems to be on the same page, and if he's not, he is willing to be curious and learn.

You can be Jeffrey or the second person. What's the articulable difference? Jeffrey is *worth knowing*. He's knowledgeable, well-read, and an interesting conversationalist because of his ability to discuss different opinions and perspectives. He's not just putting on an act; he is genuinely a curious person who thirsts for knowledge and information. These are likable qualities that we seek out in others.

Here we have another straightforward principle. The principle of worthiness is that, to be likable, you should be a person worth liking. It sounds cyclical, but it's a truism that we never think about. Likable people are likable for a reason. They are interesting, positive, knowledgeable, charming, or any other number of positive traits. What positive traits do *you* possess that would make you likable? You don't have to be knowledgeable and curious like Jeffrey, but being likable is much easier when you possess traits worthy of being liked. There is no substitute.

A more succinct way to put it is this that you should become the type of person you would like to get to know. What kind of person do you seek out? Cultivate habits and behaviors and improve yourself so that you are exactly who you would find likable instead of pretending or relying on party tricks.

You'll hear similar advice when you enter the dating advice genre—people play games and use tricks such as waiting a few days to return a call or pretending to be busier than they really are. This is all a ruse designed to make people appear attractive and busy, but in reality, people could just spend their time becoming that person they are pretending to be. Likability will come much more easily if you simply become a likable version of yourself (eventually) instead of memorizing an action plan for likability.

It's easier than it sounds because we know there are certain traits and behaviors that are more likable than others. If you're likable, you generally have the ability to introduce people to new knowledge or experiences. Think about Jeffrey from the above example—you preferred him over the other person because he was able to introduce something to your life. You prefer someone who actively skydives over someone who watches television all day. You prefer someone who has something to teach you in an interesting subject.

Therefore, this chapter focuses on ways to have interesting knowledge and also create memorable experiences with people. If you get rid of notions such as wanting to impress people or be perceived in a certain way, you'll quickly find that the process of becoming able to introduce people to new things produces a very likable person. It leads to someone who is worthy of being liked just on account of what he does.

Pursue and Act

Someone who is worthy of being liked has their own life and pursues what they want.

Sitting at home, working 24/7, or always talking about the same things won't make you interesting. In fact, it makes you seem like you have nothing going on in your life, and that may be an accurate assessment. Everyone has everyday experiences and isn't interested in rehashing them with others. Most likely, when people ask you what you have been up to, they don't want to hear you say "work."

They may laugh and smile, but the conversation stops there because they know any other details from you will probably be boring. But imagine how you could get the conversation to take outrageous twists and turns if you said something else, like "I went skydiving. It was so exhilarating, dropping fourteen thousand through the air! My chute almost didn't deploy but it finally did—phew!" Imagine the questions and comments people would have—but the point here is that you cared enough to take initiative and pursue an interest of yours, not that you are bragging about something you did. That's a worthy trait, and it results in more engagement and people taking interest in you. If someone asked you about your weekend, and your honest answers provoke those types of responses in people, then you're on the right track.

Maybe jumping out of planes is not your cup of tea—that's fine, too. You just need to find things that you have an interest in and take steps toward quenching that interest. You can later impart new knowledge to people, or you might find people who share the hobby with you and want to do it with you in the future.

The more interests you have, the more interesting you become. When you're engaged, you're engaging. These adages don't just sound clever; they ring true. People take an interest in those doing worthwhile things with their lives. It's likable. You are also more likely to find someone who shares one or more of your hobbies. If you just have one single hobby, people will quickly find you boring because the odds of them sharing that hobby are somewhat slim and because you offer little to talk about.

Imagine if all you talked about was collecting *Star Wars* action figures. Other than the occasional fanatic who also shares your hobby, most people won't be able to relate and won't find your conversation very interesting. They will like you less and avoid you when they realize that 1970s mint-condition Darth Vader dolls are all that you talk about and thus they cannot relate to you on any level or find things to talk with you about that they care about. But if you also are into painting, you can find more people who enjoy that and you can appeal to a larger demographic of people because you don't just have that one single odd hobby that few others share with you. You're just increasing your surface area of being interesting and engaging.

This all carries into the idea that you should avoid being one-dimensional. I once had a boss whose sole interest, purpose, and passion in life was sports. That's it. The guy couldn't carry conversation like a normal person unless the topic related to sports. Or if the conversation was not about sports, he'd go out of his way to make sure it slowly became that way. This put off people who didn't like or care about sports. It also prevented him from getting involved in conversations that didn't involve sports, which limited what he could talk about and who he could talk to. Most people felt annoyed by him and even people who liked sports found his extremism obnoxious, annoying, and off-putting.

Avoid being like my boss. People are interested in people who have interests, and doubly so in people who pursue those interests. To that end, always try to have something you are working on or toward—a project in your free time unrelated to work and unrelated to passive consumption of media via some type of screen. You don't have to set the bar to loving a passion, but rather just investigating something you are interested in.

You will enjoy life more, learn a lot, and have more to talk about. Others will want to talk about your project and ask questions. Your new endeavor might also expose you to new people who share this endeavor, allowing you to broaden your social horizons.

You might consider learning a foreign language, which allows you to meet other people who speak that language and form friendships with them. You might consider building model cars, planes, or trains and joining a club for that. You might fix up an old junk car and get it in cherry condition and go to car shows on the weekends. You might get into landscaping, or grow your own food, or create a koi fish pond, or take up painting or yoga. Do martial arts and work your way up to a black belt or even pursue a new career.

In the movie *Yes Man*, Jim Carrey is forced to start saying yes to everything—literally everything. As a result, his life is transformed and he has many unforgettable experiences that he would never have had otherwise. He meets the love of his life, goes on many adventures, and other such things.

Well, you need to be like his character and get into the habit of just saying yes and never saying no. Cease the overthinking and giving yourself excuses to say no. You don't even need a reason to say yes, so saying yes should become very easy and automatic for you. Simply ask "Why not?" to kill the overthinking and go along with a new experience. Don't set expectations for what happens. Just be curious about what will happen and have an open mind.

Don't be so picky as to your standards for entertainment and pleasure and comfort. It won't meet your standards but you can still gain some sort of benefit or joy from it. All change has the potential to be uncomfortable at first—sometimes the most uncomfortable situations can make for great stories later. Imagine telling people about sleeping in a roach-infested hostel in Bangkok or losing all of your luggage and having to make do.

You may have to take initiative in creating a schedule that is about pursuit and action. As long as you experiment with something new weekly or even monthly, your life will become filled with amazing new things you can talk about. You can also put yourself in the path of new people you normally would never meet in your usual routine, which can help you make more friends as a result.

The key here is to engage in what interests you with reckless abandon. Step out of the comfort zone to do new things that you might even be afraid of. To truly be more interesting, include other people in your new experiences. Enable and egg others on to become part of other people's interesting stories as well. You might want to invite someone to join you zip-lining, or invite someone to make a craft with you, or go out to eat at a new ethnic restaurant, or take a road trip.

Sharing experiences with others adds a more dynamic flair to their own lives. And they have you to thank. They will find you more interesting and they will enjoy talking about their interesting experiences with you for years to come.

The possibilities are endless—just commit and pursue, at least for a little while. This may sound like a lot of work, but what if you just replaced a fraction of the countless hours you waste on social media with reading and researching about a new area of study? When someone we meet at a party has a notable hobby or a high level of achievement in anything, we are instantly captivated. They are worthy of being liked, at least initially, and that can easily be you.

Think More

One huge part of being likable is sharing knowledge. I'll never forget a child who sat down next to me at an old job and said, "Do you know what an elephant's pubic hair is called? It's called a dude." (I later found out this was an accurate fact.) This kid gripped me with both his outrageous assertion and his sense of humor. We became work buddies. The same concept comes into play in any conversation or interaction with a new person. You don't necessarily need to know and learn more for the sake of shocking people with new facts, but it is undeniably beneficial to how people view you. The more you know, the more you can talk about, and the more ways you can connect.

This is really a point on educating yourself more and proactively gaining knowledge instead of relying on it to come to you passively. Be more well-read. You would be amazed what you can learn from books or even just newspapers five minutes a day. Being able to explain how things work, how things relate to each other, or what unique phenomena are also enlightens others and makes you more interesting.

If you have little to say, that means you need to consume more in general and gain perspective outside of your everyday existence.

The more you have to talk about, the better. This does not mean that you ought to be starting a conversation with someone and running through a handful of topics one after another, but the more knowledgeable you are of different things, the better the chances are that you and your conversation partner will connect and see eye to eye on something. You want to aim for breadth and touch on many topics as opposed to depth and delving deeply into one sole topic. The act of knowing is more than simply being interesting—it makes conversation with you easy and, oftentimes, a delight. It allows you to teach, instruct, enlighten, lead, and always have something interesting to say.

Develop and share opinions, even if you have to start by parroting other people's opinions. People love discussing opinions. Even if you disagree with someone, conversation follows. Without an opinion, conversation stalls and dies. An opinion shows that you are interested, that you have made some sort of decision based on the facts you have, and that you are active in thinking about the world as a whole. Just imagine how frustrating it is to ask someone where they want to eat for dinner, but they never have an answer. Don't be that person.

Imagine this. You bring up Brexit and you expect the other person to respond to you about it. But the other person has nothing to say. With a shrug, all he says is "Oh, yeah, I heard about that." His lack of an opinion where you expect one freezes the conversation. There is nothing else to talk about as that topic has been killed and now you don't want to start a new topic because you are afraid he will shoot that one down, too. You would be far more interested if you met someone who had a clear opinion on Brexit and was able to discuss it with you. A lack of opinion simply makes it seem like you don't think about things.

Not everyone has had tons of life experience or exposure to the news. But everyone has the ability to be curious about new things and care to learn. Having the curiosity to care about other people and new things will make others want to talk to you and explain things to you or teach you new ideas. Your curiosity will create likability by itself.

The benefit to you is obvious. You are making yourself a more well-rounded and likable person when you use intellectual curiosity to discover and learn. Imagine how you can broaden your life and your mind by learning about new things whenever you have the chance, and imagine how many people will be eager to teach you about things they really care about. You are killing two birds with one stone.

Intellectual curiosity compels you to explore the world, both around you and the world away from you that requires a 16-hour flight to explore. You don't have to fly to another country to learn a new language, meet new people, and try exotic food. From home, you can broaden your horizons, become more engaged in the world around you, and thus become more interesting. All you need to do is take the first step and learn.

The benefit in likability to others is also massive. If someone asks you what you think about fishing, and you have never gone, you would shut the conversation down if you just said, "I don't fish." What if you expressed intellectual curiosity instead? For instance, "I haven't gone fishing before, but it sounds interesting. Why do you like fishing? What's your favorite part about it?" There's an element about this that opens people up to you, so inviting them to impart knowledge to you will tickle them and lead to a great conversation.

Takeaways:

- The principle of worthiness can be confusing at first because it sounds like circular reasoning. To be more likable, you should make yourself worthy of being likable, and that involves transforming yourself into the type of person you would seek out. If you honestly appraise yourself right now, you might find that this is not the case. Therefore, make yourself *worthy*.
- Making yourself worthy is a facet of *The more interests you have, the more interesting you become* and *When you're engaged, you're engaging.* Pursue your

interests with reckless abandon to become worthy of being liked and admired. Take action to differentiate yourself in a way that satisfies your desires and jump out of your comfort zone to do it. One-dimensionality is not a favorable trait; we don't seek people out who have no hobbies and nothing they are passionate about or working toward.

- Making yourself worthy is not only about action; it is about thought. Simply put, you probably need to think and read more. Stop relying on information to passively come to you; proactively learn about what you are interested in. Have intellectual curiosity. Develop opinions by thinking through different perspectives and become more knowledgeable in general. When you are more well-read and think more deeply, and pursue your interests and act upon them with reckless abandon, you start to turn into someone that is truly likable and captivating.

Cheat Sheet

Chapter 1: The Principle of Deciding to Be Friends

- A highly underrated facet of being likable is the simple decision to treat people like friends instead of like strangers. It sounds small, but it affects everything you say or do toward people. This chapter is about making that conscious choice and realizing that you aren't doing it.

- When you make the decision, you might also realize how passive you generally are in regards to seeking out new people. This might be because of fear of judgment and rejection. But rejection and judgment are far away due to reciprocity and reciprocity of liking. The mere exposure effect also helps, as there is a clear linear relationship between time spent with someone and overall affection for them.

- Therefore, we must usually be the first person to spring into action, because others aren't conditioned to, which leads to a stalemate of each party waiting for the other to act first. You have to take initiative and be the initiator and planner, at least at first. Be specific with your plan, make it easy for them, and be comfortable going out without others.

Chapter 2: The Principle of Self-Disclosure

- The principle of self-disclosure is a surprising one because it makes most people uncomfortable at first. But realizing that TMI is a powerful weapon in finding connection points with people can push most through the zone of discomfort. The truth is, sharing more about your emotions, life stories, and experiences will help you connect with people because they are universal. Plus, sharing more makes people judge and stereotype you less.

- When you disclose more, you are able to find similarities more easily with people, and similarity is a precursor to comfort, which is a precursor to likability. Of course, you want to share relatively slowly at first so you can gauge people's response.
- We know we should disclose more, and once we get into the habit, it's not that difficult. But what about compelling other people to reciprocate, which they may or may not always do? Sure, you can talk about their interests, stroke their ego, or ask better questions, but a better method is to use elicitation. Elicitation is using indirect phrasing to make people feel like they need to speak up at that very moment.
- Types of elicitation include recognition and praise, complaining and sharing of negative emotions, making people correct you, self-effacement, naïveté, shifting the window, provocative statements, and silence.

Chapter 3: The Principle of Safety and Comfort

- This chapter is focused on being predictable—in a good way. When you're predictable in a good way, it means people feel comfortable around you and aren't worried that you are going to throw a temper tantrum on them. It allows people to feel okay with letting their guards down.
- The first way to create a safe and comforting presence is to learn negative emotion management. This is where you learn to deal with negativity, criticism, being wrong, and not taking things out on other people.
- Being transparent is another way to make people feel safe. When you're transparent, people don't feel like you're hiding something or using them for some nefarious purpose. You can create this feeling when you're relatively free with information, not evasive, and consistent with how you present yourself to different people.
- Don't be judgmental. Everyone has flaws, which is a concept repeated by the Japanese theory of wabi sabi;

imperfection is the very thing that makes something beautiful and unique. Furthermore, vulnerability has been shown to be likable and charming as seen by the Pratfall effect.

- Overall, just make someone's day and be intentional about it. You probably don't think this way because you're thinking about yourself most of the time, but taking in this mindset makes it extremely clear how to be more likable for others.

Chapter 4: The Principle of Listening

- The principle of listening well is one that you always hear or read about but probably don't actually engage in. That's because most advice on listening is simply to listen more. That's only part of it.
- To listen better, you should practice your responsiveness. Listening is not a passive activity, and responsiveness is what happens after you process what you have heard. Optimal responsiveness consists of understanding, validating,

and caring. The best singular way to demonstrate responsiveness is to ask questions.

- Listening is a fantastic method of gathering information about yourself. When you observe and monitor others, you gain self-awareness because you can understand how you are being received in multiple facets. Use other people like a mirror to see yourself.

- Validation is another powerful aspect of listening. Validation is when you subtly say, "I see your emotion, share it, and understand it." This is best demonstrated with validating statements, which are emotion-focused, and eliminating invalidating statements, which are incredibly common and serve to dismiss people's emotions.

- Finally, listen with intent to listen better.

Chapter 5: The Principle of Being Valuable

- The principle of being valuable can sound insensitive and transactional, but it simply plays on the fact that humans

ⵜⵯⴻ ⵓⴹⴰⴱⵏⵓ

BUSINESS REPLY MAIL

FIRST-CLASS MAIL PERMIT NO. 54 BOONE IA

POSTAGE WILL BE PAID BY ADDRESSEE

THE WEEK

PO BOX 37251
BOONE IA 50037-2251

THE WEEK | Just $1.98 an issue!

☐ **YES!** Send me 50 issues (1 year) of THE WEEK for just $99.
I'll save 60% off the single copy rate. *That's like getting 30 issues free!*

☐ I prefer 25 issues for $59

60% OFF

Name _____
(please print)

Address _____

City _____ State _____ Zip _____

Email address _____

☐ Payment enclosed   ☐ Bill me

order online: theweek.com/exclusive

are selfish creatures. We are, initially at least, motivated to spend time with those who we perceive as valuable. Value isn't just money-related, thank goodness.

- Being valuable is about how to be helpful and add to people's lives and impart positive feelings. You can do this by addressing people's practical needs and desires or their emotional needs and desires. The realistic way of doing this is to think about five-minute favors for people.

- Additional ways of adding value are being a social connector, being the planner of a group, and focusing on providing entertainment (in the same way that people enjoy going to a movie).

- This principle underscores an important theme of considering others and not approaching people from a self-centered perspective.

Chapter 6: The Principle of Shallowness

- This is a principle about our sad reality. We are shallow creatures, though we might not like to admit it or play the game. Thus, how can we shore up our physical appearance and make a better shallow impression?

- Studies have identified at least six judgments people make based purely on physical appearance such as having a "baby face," an easy gait, dressing well, and speaking quickly. Studies also showed that it depends on who you are talking to in terms of relative status. If you are talking to someone of lower status, a better impression will depend on appearing nice. If you are talking to someone of higher status, a better impression will depend on appearing competent.

- Vocal pitch has also been shown to make a difference, impression-wise. A higher-pitched voice has been associated with trustworthiness, while a lower-pitched voice has been associated with authority and leadership.

- This should come as no surprise; a handshake's characteristics are used to stereotype and judge—at least in Western cultures. Finally, wardrobe can make a difference as to how you are perceived. Dressing too well or too poorly can open a can of worms; thus, it is a good policy to dress similarly to who you want to make an impression on so you can get the benefit of the doubt.

Chapter 7: The Principle of Empathy

- The principle of empathy is the principle of understanding people's emotional states, the causes, and how you have the potential to contribute negatively or positively. For our purposes, emotional intelligence is mostly interchangeable. Emotional intelligence is similarly about the understanding of causes of emotions in all parties present and consists of self-awareness, self-management, social awareness, and social management.
- Empathy is important because it allows you to generate positive and likable outcomes with people on account of understanding their mental states of being. There are a few ways to grow your powers of empathy. These include focusing on what is good for others,

thinking about shared values and experiences, not judging others, stepping into other people's perspective and unique set of circumstances, asking open-ended questions to gather information, self-disclosing, using neutral ground and creating an optimal space for sharing, not jumping to the end of the conversation, and practicing it until it becomes an unconscious habit.

Chapter 8: The Principle of Abrasiveness

- Although it may not seem like it, this is an extremely important chapter. Sometimes it pays to be less abrasive and annoying than charming. Charming may open doors for you, but being abrasive and unlikable will shut them even more quickly.
- Most of the ways we are abrasive and unlikable are relatively indirect. They are actions that make people want to avoid us and stop contact. One such way is maintaining one-sided relationships in terms of effort, emotional support, and time invested. If this occurs, then you

may become known as someone who reaches out only when they want something: a user. Be sure to proactively provide emotional support to others, especially if you have just unloaded your emotions onto someone else.

- Recognize that everyone has different limitations and don't overstay your welcome. This applies to all avenues but especially social appetites and desire for interaction. Everyone has their own boundaries, so don't try to force past them because you'll only be met with annoyance and resentment.

- Finally, use the THINK acronym to evaluate your words and their impact on people to not be abrasive. THINK stands for True, Helpful, Inspiring, Necessary, and Kind. Get into the habit of running your thoughts through this type of filter for increased likability.

Chapter 9: The Principle of Worthiness

- The principle of worthiness can be confusing at first because it sounds like

205

circular reasoning. To be more likable, you should make yourself worthy of being likable, and that involves transforming yourself into the type of person you would seek out. If you honestly appraise yourself right now, you might find that this is not the case. Therefore, make yourself *worthy*.

- Making yourself worthy is a facet of *The more interests you have, the more interesting you become* and *When you're engaged, you're engaging.* Pursue your interests with reckless abandon to become worthy of being liked and admired. Take action to differentiate yourself in a way that satisfies your desires and jump out of your comfort zone to do it. One-dimensionality is not a favorable trait; we don't seek people out who have no hobbies and nothing they are passionate about or working toward.

- Making yourself worthy is not only about action; it is about thought. Simply put, you probably need to think and read more. Stop relying on information to passively come to you; proactively learn about what you are interested in. Have intellectual curiosity. Develop opinions by thinking through different perspectives and become more knowledgeable in general. When you are more well-read and think more deeply, and pursue your interests and act upon them with reckless abandon, you start to turn into someone that is truly likable and captivating.

Made in the USA
Middletown, DE
06 January 2020

82666797R00117